SELECTED ARTICLES ON

ENTERPRISE RESOURCES PLANNING (ERP)

VOLUME I

V K RAMASWAMY (RAM)

About the author

Ever since he created the first inventory transaction in ERP back in 1998, Ramaswamy (Ram) had marvelled at the potential of ERP – to improve societal efficiencies by optimizing material consumption, to help fight climate change by making the office paperless and to bring down the disputes between entities (thus create more happier universe) through effective documentation and timely communication.

A graduate in Mechanical Engineering from the prestigious Government Engineering College, Trichur in the beautiful state of Kerala in South India, Ram worked for 10 years as an operations engineer in Steel Authority of India in Durgapur in the state of West Bengal in India. Those gruelling years gave him domain expertise in manufacturing. Those years also taught him how to communicate with a shop floor worker, a knowledge that has helped him weather the change management challenges that are a part of ERP Implementation for manufacturing industry.

Ram has passion for continuous learning and improvement. In 1995, he took a Sabbatical to do MBA from IISWBM under Kolkata University. It was in those two years, 95-97, that Ram became passionate about accounting, a knowledge that is core for an ERP Consultant.

Two years in academia provided the conceptual rigour and theoretical foundation to his ten years of learning in the shop floor. These two years assimilated and consolidated his learning over the previous eleven years and made him ready to enter the exciting world of ERP Consulting in 2000.

Those were exciting times for ERP Consultant with solid domain expertise like what Ram had. In the ensuing years he has delivered successful ERP implementations. He was worked in different roles including Consultant, Project Manager, Solutions Architect, Program Manager and CIO. He has implemented ERP for different industries including Discrete Manufacturing, Process Manufacturing, Jewellery, Chemicals, Insurance, Pharmaceuticals, Fertilizers and Governments.

Ram has been fortunate to have worked in different countries across the world. He has implemented projects in Mexico, Colombia, USA, UK, Dubai and Bangladesh in addition to innumerable projects that he delivered in India. He has implemented solutions for all core business areas including Procurement, Materials Management, Manufacturing, Order Fulfilment, Financials, Budgeting and Financial Reporting.

He lives in Bangalore with his wife Jyoti and his mother. His son, Aditya is pursuing his graduation in Computer Science from BITS, Pilani in the state of Rajasthan.

His passions are ERP, Self Improvement and Investing. He is a passionate blogger managing three blogs, one on each of his interest areas.

Ram loves to communicate. He can be contacted on:

Email: vkrama01@gmail.com
Phone: +91 98801 79317 / 86183 24497
Twitter: @vkrama01

Skype:	vkrama
LinkedIn:	https://www.linkedin.com/in/vkramaswamy/
ERP Blog:	http://erp-consultancy.blogspot.in

"DEDICATED TO THE WONDERFUL,
EXCITING AND CHALLENGING
PROFESSION OF ERP CONSULTING"

About the book

I have been fortunate to have been working in the field of ERP (Enterprise Resources Planning) from 1998. I started my career as an ERP consultant in the year 2000. From 2000 to 2004, I worked on an ERP Application named SCALA. I was a part of 5 SCALA implementations in the role of consultant and project manager. SCALA is a single consultant implementation, one consultant has to implement all the process flows including, P2P, C2V, S2B, O2C, A2D and R2R. Working on SCALA gave me a complete view of ERP Implementation. Since the product was rigid and could not be customized I developed the habit of delivering amazing work arounds to customer's unique requirements.

In the year 2004, I moved to Oracle Applications.

The second project in this product was a very complex one and quickly catapulted me to an expert on Oracle Process Manufacturing and Costing. I am one of the few consultants to have implemented all the types of costing methods including Standard Costing, Average Costing and Specific Costing. My domain experience, my knowledge of accounting and knowledge of ERP applications and finally the deep expertise in implementing ERP gives me an edge I think.

I have been working on Oracle Applications ever since. I have worked on different types of engagements including implementations, application development and ERP Upgrades.

In the year 2007, I started writing on topics related to ERP. I posted three white papers in IT Tool Box and started my blog in the same year. Since then I have written more than 200 posts in my ERP Blog, almost one post a month on an average.

This book is a collection of selected articles posted in my blog between 2007 and 2010. As I reviewed those posts to be included in this book, I modified and added more content and also added images to improve the look and feel. All the articles, except one, are universal.

This is the first edition of this book. I am sure there are obvious errors that I have missed out. Do let me know if you find any errors.

The objective of this book is to add value to the knowledge of ERP in the world. Let us do it together.

Thank you for reading this book, Please share your feedback so that I can improve upon it

Ram

TABLE OF CONTENTS

ABOUT THE AUTHOR..2
ABOUT THE BOOK 6
ERP CONCEPTS 9
   7 FLOWS TO BE CONSIDERED IN AN ERP IMPLEMENTATION 10
   FOREIGN CURRENCY TRANSACTION CONCEPTS...................................21
   INVENTORY VALUATION / COSTING CHALLENGES IN AN ERP IMPLEMENTATION..........24
ERP DESIGN..35
   DESIGN ERP TO CREATE A 'LEAN' ORGANIZATION.....................................36
   TOWARDS GLOBAL CHART OF ACCOUNTS (GLOBAL COA) 57
   DESIGN CONSIDERATIONS IN SET OF BOOKS 70
   DESIGN CONSIDERATIONS FOR ITEM CODING 73
   EFFECTIVE USE OF EXCEPTION REPORTING IN ERP IMPLEMENTATION 80
DATA MIGRATION...83
   DATA MIGRATION STRATEGIES IN ERP 84
   INTAKE OF OPENING BALANCE 101
ERP IMPLEMENTATION 107
   SOLUTION ARCHITECTURE FOR ERP IMPLEMENTATION 108
   ERP JOURNEY - 10 RISKS FACED BY AN SME 124
   PRODUCT DEMO: A GREAT WAY TO INTRODUCE YOUR TEAM................................132
   DELIVERING HEALTHY PROJECTS: MY VIEW 136
   REQUIREMENT GATHERING: THE PAIN IN A CONSULTANT'S LIFE.............................141
   ANALYTICAL V/S TRANSACTIONAL INFORMATION IN AN ERP IMPLEMENTATION 144
INDIA LOCALIZATION...149
   TDS FLOW IN ACCOUNTS PAYABLE - ORACLE APPS INDIA LOCALIZATION 150
GENERAL..156
   KEY SKILLS OF A GOOD ERP CONSULTANT...157
   EVERY JOB HAS TO BE DONE TWICE..160
   DOCUMENT CHANGE HISTORY 164

ERP CONCEPTS

7 Flows to be considered in an ERP implementation

Introduction
A functional consultant going to a customer site to implement an ERP solution need to have a clear and structured idea of the various aspects of the business. An ERP implementation can be successful only if it is done top down. This means that the consultant has to identify the business processes, issues and constraint before he gets down to the task of designing the solution. One way to do this is to start with the key reports that the organization is presently using and analyse as to the kind of information that is key to this organization.

To implement ERP in a structured way, one of the methods is to divide the process into various flows. There are 7 important flows that a consultant needs to understand thoroughly and integrate the same in the ERP to ensure a successful ERP implementation.

1. Business Flow:
Logically business flow encompasses all the processes being presently followed by the organization. However, from the perspective of ERP implementation, the consultant has to focus on certain key questions to understand the business thoroughly. Some the questions which should be used in this analysis are;

Organization: What is the nature of the organization? Is it distribution intensive? Does it have many depots? Franchises? Is it operations intensive? Is it purchase intensive? What is the power structure in the organization? Who is the project champion? Who could be a potential risk? What is the age profile of the users? What is the change culture of the organization? Are they comfortable with technology?

Sales: How does the customer enter the organization? What is the typical customer profile – repeat or ad hoc? Do they follow significant customer approach? Do they have separate priority for category 1 customers and another for the other types of customers? What are the criteria for deciding a customer as a category 1 customer? How frequent is the review? How does order gets registered? What are the product segments that the Organization in? What SKUs are they selling? How does Organization handle available to promise issues? Who are their top 10 Customers and what is the proportion of revenue from each? What is their credit policy? Are they operating in a buyer's market or a seller's market? Are their collections automated? Which geography do they operate in? What are the three key challenges in sales that a consultant can add value?

Procurement: Where does organization procure materials? What are the key specifications? What are the top three raw materials? How many suppliers are there for each of the critical raw materials? Will the Organization be able to withstand a supplier default? What kind of market the company operates in, buyer's or seller's? What are the three key issues in procurement where a consultant can add value?

Conversion: What is the organizations conversion process? How complex is the routing? Do they use sub-assemblies in manufacturing? How is the production planning done – manual or automated? How is production scheduling done, manual or automatic? What are the quality parameters? How is quality check done?

Inventory: How is inventory management done, for example how do they handle obsolete inventory? What is the inventory turnover ratio? What is the level of obsolete inventory in the organization? How is the quality measured? How is the material being managed? How general are the items? Can we divide the items into distinct categories? How is the material issue taking place? What is the size of inventory master? How are items coded?

Inventory valuation: What is the costing method used? Why are they using that costing method? What is the cost of items? How does the costing get done? How does the organization measure the profitability? Is it on a per order basis or a per customer basis?

Local Taxation: How is local taxation and reporting handled? What are the statutory reports to be submitted? What is the frequency of submission? How many different local authorities have to be supported? Are they using some third party application for Statutory Reporting Requirements?

ERP Implementation: What is the driver for ERP Implementation – do they have clearly identified business benefits or are they going for ERP because competitors have moved into ERP? Who drives the ERP Implementation, IT or business? Are the processes documented clearly? Are the Organizational Roles and responsibilities designed correctly?

At the end of business flow understanding, the consultant should have a clear idea of top five business reasons why the organization is going for and ERP and the key reasons for choosing this particular ERP Product. This would give the consultant a clear idea of customer expectation. Answer to the last section on 'ERP Implementation' could give you an idea of the risks involved in this implementation.

2. Process Flow:

The six key flows in a manufacturing industry are Procure to Pay (P2P), Demand to Build (D2B), Order to Cash (O2C), Costing to Inventory Valuation (C2V), Assets to depreciation (A2D) and Record to Report (R2R).

Here is a diagrammatic representation of each of these flows.

Procure to Pay (P2P)

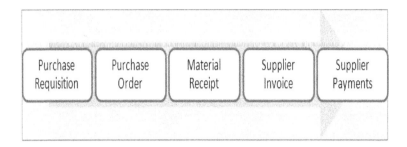

Demand to Build (D2B)

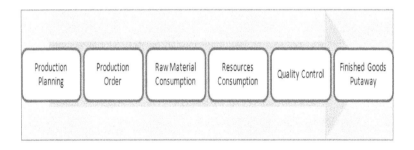

Order to Cash (O2C)

Costing to Inventory Valuation (C2V)

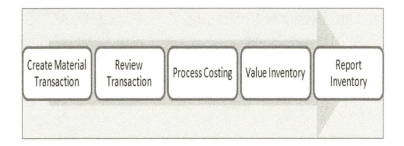

Assets to Depreciation (A2D)

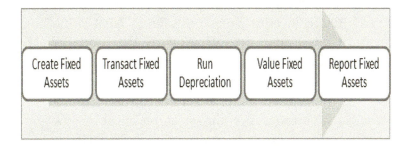

Record to Report (R2R)

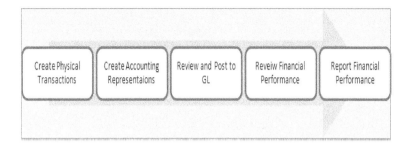

| Create Physical Transactions | Create Accounting Representaions | Review and Post to GL | Reveiw Financial Performance | Report Financial Performance |

Of course all of the above are high level process flows. Each element in the above flow has one or more detailed processes / flows attached. A consultant should understand all the above process flows at a sufficient level of detail including the accounting impact of the processes. This understanding will decide the key setups in the ERP Implementation.

3. Material Flow:
How is the material received in the organization? What are the processes to be followed at gate entry? How is it inspected and accepted into inventory? How is inventory tracked? How is inventory made obsolete? What is the process of physical inventory? What is the mode of material movement to production, is it push or pull? Is it a bulk movement or based on each production order? How does the unused material return to raw material warehouse (this process is known as backflush)? How does the finished product come into Finished Goods stores? What are the quality checks? How are quality rejects handled? How is it picked for shipping, FIFO or LIFO? How is it packed and shipped? This will give you a

clear picture of the complexity in material handling process.

4. Document Flow:

For each of the flows discussed in step 2 and 3, you need to know the associated document flows. Some of these documents are internal to the organization (inspection report, GRN etc) where data accuracy is of primary importance, while others are external to organization (PO, AR Invoice etc) where data accuracy as well as presentation are equally important. The consultant should focus more on external reports without spending too much time on the look and feel of internal reports.

The document flow in Procure to Pay (P2P) process is as follows:

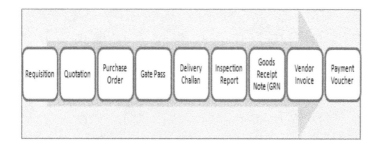

Out of these, only Purchase Order and Payment Voucher are external documents. You may say that Vendor Invoice is an external report, but that is a document that is coming in to the Organization on which the ERP Implementation has no control on.

5. Accounting Flow:

For each of the processes discussed in point 2, you need to know how the Accounting entries are generated and how they impact the profit / profitability of the organization. Please note that for every inventory transaction ERP creates an accounting entry (Perpetual inventory valuation). The consultant needs to be clear of the accounting steps. The inventory accounting has a tendency of getting out of hand. One of the key constraints in ERP is the understanding of local tax accounting flows and mapping the same. The consultant needs to allocate some time for this activity.

The Accounting Impact of Procure to Pay (P2P) process is given below as an example.

No	Process Name	Accounting Impact?	Debit	Credit
1	Create Purchase Requisition	No		
2	Create Purchase Order	No		
3	Receive Material in the Factory	Yes	Material Under Inspection Account	Accrued Purchases Account
4	Inspect Material	No		
5	Deliver Material in the Stock	Yes	Inventory Account	Material Under Inspection Account
6	Enter Supplier Invoices	Yes	Accrued Purchases Account	Creditors Account
7	Make Supplier Payments	Yes	Creditors Account	Bank Account

6. Report Flow:

You need to know the key reports in the ERP package which shows that all the above flows are functioning correctly. Some of the key reports are Inventory valuation report, Open invoices report in both Receivables and Payables, Supplier advances in Payables, Customer Advances in Receivables, both Customer and Supplier Balances reports, Assets Register, Depreciation / Accumulated Depreciation report, Supplier listing, Customer listing, Open POs, Open SOs, Trial Balance etc.

The above 6 Flows are what I call 'Above the Surface' Flows. A functional consultant needs to be clear of the above flows.

7. Data Flow:

This is the final flow that a consultant should know. Knowledge of this flow helps him to write better specifications for reports, customizations and integrations. The questions to be asked about this flow are: How the data flows through the database based on your transactions? What are the key tables? What are their linkages? How does the data flow from one process to another? How does the data flow from one process flow to another?

A consultant should strive to attain a clear understanding of the above flows. This will help her to talk the language of the client. The ability of the consultant to talk business language is very important to get the buy in from the end user, to improve the user adoption of ERP, to tailor her implementation to meet the business requirements of the organization and to have a clear assessment of the implementation risks.

Foreign Currency Transaction Concepts

There are four concepts in foreign currency transactions. They are:

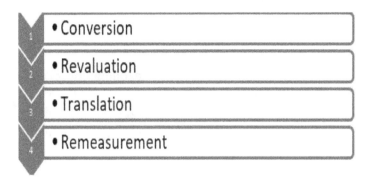

- Conversion
- Revaluation
- Translation
- Remeasurement

1. Conversion.
Conversion takes place at the time of the transaction entry and is normally done at the Spot Rate (or at the morning rate if the rates are updated every morning). For example, if an Indian company has an import payable liability of 100 USD and the exchange rate is 40 INR / 1 USD, the foreign currency payable is converted to the INR value of 4000. ERP automatically does this conversion.

2. Revaluation
This happens at the end of the period. The foreign currency account balances are revalued based on the period end exchange rate. Normally the impact goes into

'unrealized gains / losses' account. For example, if the exchange rate is 45 at the end of the period, the foreign currency payable of 100 USD is revalued to 4500 INR and the 'Unrealized Loss' in this case is Rs. 500. The accounting entry in the above case is:

| Unrealized Loss A/c | Debit | 500 |
| Liability | Credit | 500 |

The above entry is either reversed at the beginning of the next period or carried forward. The actual realized gain / loss is booked at the time of closing the above transaction, by payment against the invoice in the above example.

3. Translation

Translation is used when the organization reports in a foreign currency which is different from its base currency. This happens when a Foreign Subsidiary sends the monthly statements to its HQ. The financial statements have to be translated to the reporting currency. This process happens at the period end. In this case, the base currency trial balance is translated to the foreign currency trial balance. You can use different exchange rates to translate different account types. For example, you could use historical rates to translate owner's equity and fixed assets, the period end rates to translate current assets and liabilities and period average rates to translate income statement accounts.

4. Remeasurement

This happens in situations where the base currency is an inflationary currency. In this case the parent will want to keep a close track of the transactions by remeasuring every transaction in the currency of parent company. For example if your base currency is Argentine Peso and the parent currency is USD, every transaction in Argentine Peso will be remeasured in USD in the day's exchange rate. This ensures a tight control by parent on the subsidiary's operations and provides the parent with a real time report of the subsidiary's financial performance. This helps effective intervention by the parent in case subsidiary's performance deteriorates due to domestic inflation.

Inventory Valuation / Costing Challenges in an ERP Implementation

Introduction:

One of the key challenges in an ERP Implementation is the identification of the correct costing method to be used to get the maximum benefit to the organization. Most of the time, the selection of costing method is determined by the Consultant's familiarity with a particular costing methodology and not out of any specific organizational costing or inventory valuation challenges. In addition, most of the costing consultants are not aware of the accounting impact of their decisions. And finally, despite the fact that the costing process is an inherently 'averaging' activity, many consulting teams spent considerable amount of time debating on the 'most accurate' costing method.

I start off this article by describing the various costing methods used. In this section, I will try to cover as many points as possible regarding the business benefits and disadvantages of each of the methodologies. In addition, costing being a performance evaluation criterion for different departments of the organization, I will also throw some light on the various incentives perspectives related to different methods. From there I move on to describe what I call as a 'Costing Continuum' with

Specific costing at one end and standard costing at the other end.

In the final section, I look at the various challenges faced by consultants with regards to costing. Costing has many impacts. It has an impact on the closing inventory valuation and by corollary, on the profit / loss of the organization. Since costing impacts the P&L statement, it is considered by many organizations to be very sensitive configuration.

Due to the incentive nature of Costing, many organizations build their bonus / incentive structure around costing. This has the impact of trying to load all the cost components on each and every unit of the finished product. This may require expertise on costing analysis and any attempt to change the costing method may be met with reluctance and even hostility by the end customer. It is very important for the consultant to navigate these challenges. Once she is able to do that, the rewards that accrue to the success of the project can be significant. My article attempts to help you succeed in your ERP Implementation.

Note: *I have implemented different costing solutions for manufacturing industry ranging from Specific costing on the one hand to Standard costing on the other with multiple methods like FIFO, PMAC etc thrown-in in between.*

Costing Methods

There are 5 Costing Methods as shown in the diagram below. They are:

1. Specific costing
2. FIFO (First In, First Out)
3. Weighted moving average methods
4. LIFO (Last In, First Out)
5. Standard Costing.

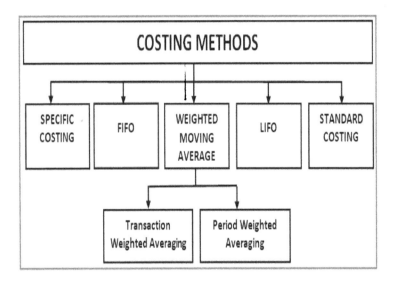

Weighted moving average methods can further be broadly classified as:

a. Transaction Moving Average Method, where the cost changes with every new receipt transaction

b. Period Moving Average Method where the cost is averaged for a specific period. The period can be a day, a week, a month or even a year.

Some of the methods above can be used only in case of discrete items (where the cost of each individual unit of the item can be clearly assigned, for example a piston), Period Moving average method is normally used if the cost of the individual unit of the item cannot be assigned (for example, milk).

While these methods are used to **assign** costs to the raw materials, they help to **calculate** the cost of the finished products. While the above difference is explainable in theory, the same difference brings in challenges in deciding the costing method. One such challenge is in make or buy situations where the costs are different for the same finished product.

Let us examine each of these methods in a little bit of detail.

1. *Specific costing:* In this costing method, the cost of each individual unit of the item is identified and assigned on the basis of the actual / specific cost incurred in procuring the same. As you can easily see, the effort required in tracking separate cost for each individual unit of the item makes this method cumbersome. This type of costing is used mostly in case of low volume, high value purchases. This method is also used when we need to track the cost of the finished good at unit /

batch / lot level. This type of costing method is used is Jewellery manufacturing industry where the cost of each unit of finished product is different from another (based on the content of gold present in the item).

2. FIFO (First In, First Out): In this costing method, it is assumed that the individual units of items are consumed in the same sequence as they are purchased. For example, the first item procured is used up first, the second item purchased is consumed next and so on. This type of costing can be used in scenarios where the item does not lose its value over time with storage and there is a regular flow of items in the warehouse. Note that, it is not necessary that the units are **actually** consumed in the same sequence of their arrival into the system, but for costing purposes it is **assumed** that the consumption pattern is the same as the receiving pattern.

As you can see, FIFO method is less accurate than specific costing. Also, in times of inflation, FIFO method will show lower cost of consumption and will inflate the profit. Since the calculated profit has a taxation impact, the companies may be averse to show inflated profit in their books. This is an impact the consultant has to consider while recommending a costing decision.

3. *Weighted Moving Average Methods:* In weighted moving average methods, the cost of the item is calculated based on a formula which considers the quantity as weight. In this method, based on every transaction of the item, the cost of the item will get updated with the latest cost. The formula used is (Current Quantity X Current Cost + New Quantity X New Cost) / (Current Quantity + New Quantity). The weighted average cost method overcomes the drawback of FIFO method of not considering the inflation in Costing. Weighted average method reflects the market cost better than FIFO.

There are two methods of Averaging the cost. In the Transaction Moving Average Method, the cost of the units is updated based on each receipt transaction (this is the example given in the previous paragraph). In Period Moving Average method, the procurements of the period are aggregated and the cost of the item for the period reflects the cost of all the purchases of that item in that period.

4. LIFO (Last In, First Out): LIFO method is not used in India. This method assumes that the items which were received last, are consumed first. (While formally this method is not used in Indian accounting system, this method is widely used in the Vegetable market in India. All the consumers want 'Fresh' stocks and the price of all the vegetables are updated with the latest cost. Classic LIFO). As can be seen, this method approaches closest to the current cost. It should also be mentioned that in times of deflation (or recession) this method inflates the profit and thereby the tax outflow. This is a double whammy for the organizations since in these periods the revenue also will be hit and organization ends up paying higher tax on lower revenue.

5. *Standard Costing:* The drawback with the methods discussed above is that they focus on **accurately recording** the cost information and hence there is **less emphasis on analysis.** In addition, all these methods calculate the costs post facto. This is where Standard Costing comes in.

In standard costing, the cost of the item is fixed for a given period based on historical analysis of the costs. Since the costs are fixed, the emphasis shifts to analysis of Variance. This means that whenever the actual cost shifts from the standard cost, the reasons for the variance are identified and corrective actions quickly taken. The corrective action could either be a process change or if the variance is directional in nature, the Standard cost itself is changed in the next period to reflect the change.

Standard costing has many advantages. First, the cost information is used for analysis purposes, which is as it should be. To record the costs post facto, as other methods do, is just a mechanical activity and do not benefit the organization. Also, Standard costing, based on its emphasis on analysis, helps to identify process gaps and helps the organization to fill these gaps effectively leading to cost optimization. On the flip side, standard costing calls for detailed knowledge of the method and analytical tools.

Note that if the cost of raw materials and resources fluctuate around a mean, there is not much difference between Standard Costing and Actual Costing. In fact, I know of organizations that use Actual Costing, but use the previous periods cost for analysis purposes (like in standard costing).

If the consultant knows the method and organization is ready for it, Standard costing can be a powerful tool for cost analysis and optimization.

Factors to be considered while deciding on a costing method

1. What is the impact on P&L:

Every costing decision has two impacts. One is a balance sheet impact showing the value of the closing inventory. Second is a P&L impact, showing the Cost of goods sold and thereby the operating profit. For the same revenue, if the closing inventory value increases, the operating profit of the company increases. Costing method changes during an ERP implementation. This will lead to a P&L impact. An implementation consultant should be very clear about the impact on P&L due to ERP implementation. Any impact on the P&L could have implication for audit & taxation and for Shareholder value.

2. What is the impact on data entry?

Any packaged application works on the principle of GIGO (Garbage In, Garbage Out). For the consistent and correct calculation of costs, accurate cost of material and resource usage has to be entered in the system. While it sounds quite logical in practice, data entry can be very cumbersome, especially in a manufacturing industry. I have observed that in manufacturing industry, the entry of labour and overheads are the most difficult since these need to be manually entered and these tend to change over each production batch.

Consultants should suggest option to achieve a balance between the tedium of data entry and the need for effective analysis.

3. What is the costing incentive system in the organization?

Costing information is a very powerful tool. Like any other powerful tool, the effectiveness of the tool lies in the knowledge of the tool and purpose for which it is used. Costing information can be used both positively and negatively by the organizations.

Take the case of purchase price variance. Purchase price variance can be analysed in detail and the standard costs can be optimized to make it as close to the actual cost as possible. In this way the purchase price variance will decline over time. Also, this level of detailed analysis will provide the organization with a wealth of information regarding its procurement process. That is the positive use of purchase price variance.

However, many organizations use the purchase price variance to punish the purchasing manager. For example, if the supplier provides volume discount, a high level of PPV could show that the purchase manager did not make use of the volume discount facility. Or if the supplier provides early payment rebate, a high level of variance could show that the AP user did not pay promptly and this led to the firm losing the early payment rebate. In this case, the organization could use this information to punish the purchase manager or AP user respectively.

It goes without saying that in the long term, using the costing information for positive purposes can lead to lasting benefits for the organization.

4. What are the parameters in costing decision (Type of item, Volume of purchase, inflation..)

This is a difficult topic to address. For example, if the input prices are highly fluctuating, standard costing may not be of much use. If cost of the inputs vary from product to product (in precision industry or ETO industry), you are better off using the actual cost. If the purchase prices are stable, then the use of standard costs can help analyse the operational performance better than actual cost. If the number of item codes is very high, then standard costing may be very cumbersome. If the number of new items being produced are high, then again, identifying the standard costs may not be feasible.

In an inflationary economy, FIFO will show high profit and hence will lead to high taxation. Reverse will be the case with LIFO.

In case of volume of purchase is high, it is better to go with standard costing since you can track the operational performance better with this method.

Conclusion
An effectively implemented costing methodology can provide rich dividends to the organization in the form of valuable analytical data which can help improve operational effectiveness and increase profitability. It is the kind of intellectual challenge and the intellectual value add that you can give to an organization that makes 'Costing' an exciting area to work on.

ERP DESIGN

Design ERP to create a 'Lean' Organization

Introduction

The concept of 'Lean' is the adaptation of Toyota Production System into western manufacturing processes. The lean involves elimination of any non-value adding activities to ensure that the customer pays for only value adding features in the product. The five principles identified in Lean are:

1. Specify what creates value from Customer's perspective
2. Identify all the steps along the process chain
3. Make those processes flow
4. Customer Pull rather than stock push
5. Continuous removal of wastes.

The principle of Lean identifies 7 wastes. These are:

1. Over Production
2. Over stocking of inventory
3. Waste of transportation
4. Processing wastes
5. Waste of idle time
6. Waste of operator time
7. Waste due to bad quality

While the above wastes are related to manufacturing processes, there are many hidden, unidentified wastes in an organization. Most of the time, these wastes are generated due too years of suboptimal business practices.

This article is divided into three sections. In the first section of this article I point out some of the non-manufacturing wastes that keep piling up over the years and make the organization suboptimal. I follow this up with some design considerations that the ERP Implementation Consultant can use to ensure an optimal, high class ERP Implementations. And in the third and final section, I illustrate the implementation of these design considerations by focusing on Oracle General Ledger module as an example.

Various Wastes in any organization

Years and years of inefficient business practices lead an organization to progressively perform at a suboptimal level. These practices lead to many wastes in the organization, none of which are related to manufacturing processes, and which together make the organization slow, lethargic and perform at a lower potential. Some of these wastes include,

1. *Waste related to Obsolete data:* The record books of most of the organizations are teeming with reams of obsolete data. The data gets piled up over a period of time, year after year, without the organization not even being aware of the piled up data. Examples include Obsolete stock, Inactive suppliers, Inactive customers, Delayed (and sometimes Forgotten!!) receivables, Delayed payments which has incurred late payment penalty, Open Purchase Orders without any transactions, Inactive Customers data etc.

2. Waste related to bad naming conventions: Sometimes badly designed naming convention can cause wasteful data. I have seen same customer created by different users in the same organization. While one created customer as XYZ Ltd, another created as XYZ Ltd. And another created as XYZ Limited! This happens because the organizations do not have a well designed naming convention in place, and even if a naming convention is available, there is no disciplined process to ensure that it is closely followed. If we can design naming conventions properly, searching of data becomes easier and faster. For example, it is faster for the system to index and retrieve numerical data rather than alphabetical data.

3. Waste due to data duplication: In many an organization, different systems exist in silos leading to data duplication. The same data with minimal variation in the details exist in multiple systems. If you take supplier master data for example, a supplier exist in the Procurement System, the same supplier exists in the receiving system and finally same supplier exists in the financial systems. This is like the proverbial story of blind men and the elephant.

Another example of data duplication is in the Finance department. Different sections need different variants of the same data. For example, a payable accountant wants to know the pending invoices and payments from the 'Due Date' perspective, the legal department wants to know the details from the 'Vendor Dispute Redressing' perspective and finally the general accounts department wants the same data from the reconciliation perspective. Since these departments do not talk to each other, the data duplicates and multiples within the organization. Most of the times, they present different picture altogether!!

4. ***Waste due to excessive transactions:*** Many a time, an organization indulges in wasteful manual transactions. For example, in many organizations, Bank Reconciliation is a manual activity. So are Vendor Payments. Most of the ERPs provide facility to easily automate these manual transactions thereby saving lot of energy, time and money to the organization.

5. ***Waste due to Excessive usage of Paper:*** Many 'Old Economy' companies, even now, demand that all the auditable transactions be accompanied by copies of physical documents and reports. An ERP can easily automate these processes thereby leading to a 'Paperless' organization.

6.   *Waste of manual labour:* An offshoot of the manual process is the need of personnel to carry physical documents from one location to another. The reason is the physical requirement of multiple data verification coupled with the Silos approach that we discussed earlier.

7.   *Wastes related to bad Account Payable Practices*: Procuring stuff and making payments to suppliers is a normal practice for any organization. Supplier returns is a major component of the Procurement cycle. Supplier Returns (also known as Return to Vendor or RTV) transactions are often accompanied by a Debit Note, which is a claim on the vendor. In many organizations, Vendor payments and Debit Note generation go on in parallel, with One Hand (which enters Supplier Payments) not knowing what the other hand (which enters Debit Notes) is doing. This leads to excessive Cash Outflow to the organization which in turn leads to requirement for additional expensive Working Capital.

8.   *Wastes due to handling customer disputes*: When the customer sends the cheques to you, the same is received in the mail receiving section. The same is then transferred to the Finance and Accounts section (through a Peon, another waste!!) and finally the same is netted off against the corresponding Customer Invoices.

There are multiple situations in the above communications chain that can lead to customer disputes and a dissatisfied customer. For example, the mail gets lost in the mail receiving section itself. Or the peon could deliver it to the wrong section where it lies unattended. Or the cheque is delivered to the right person, but he delayed or missed reconciling the receipts against the invoices in the system. Or there is no reconciliation process in the system at all. Or, the cheque was not accompanied by the invoice (an Orphan Cheque, my coinage) and hence the F&A section delayed the reconciliation...

What happens?

In the next round of the 'Dunning Cycle' a strong mail goes to the customer that his payments are pending. Customer in turn sends back the copy of your receipt acknowledgement or his bank statement showing that Cheque or Money was already received by you and gives you a sage advice to 'Get your things in order'.

Or he will consider you as a risk to do business with and leave you in favour of your competitor.

The wastes go on....

Point to note is that all the wastes that I have mentioned above relate to processes other than manufacturing.

These system and process related wastes are mostly invisible and hence get ignored by the system. Just like a lingering pain in your shoulder that make you ineffective in performing some tasks effectively, these wastes gradually pile up and increases the costs to the organization.

An intelligent and efficient ERP Design can handle all the wastes mentioned above. When we talk of 'Lean' we think of manufacturing processes and tasks relating to manufacturing and inventory. However, any process improvement which can lead to process efficiencies and lowering of costs to the customer can be considered as 'Lean' process. And in this endeavour there are many a tasks that an ERP consultant can implement. In the following section, I discuss some of the ERP Design considerations that can help reduce the wastes and bring much more flexibility and agility to the process system.

How can we design ERP to handle the above wastes?

By focusing more on issues and problems and less on requirements, a smart consultant can identify design opportunities in ERP to reduce organizational waste. Given below are some of the design considerations that, if followed, can lead to optimal ERP Design. While most of the points being discussed are ERP Vendor Agnostic, some of the terminology being used is related to Oracle Apps.

1. *Design to handle Obsolete / Redundant data*: Most of the time, an ERP Implementation leads to identification of a number of obsolete data. The design to reduce wastes cuts across all phases and all the ERP related activities. For example, customer should be encouraged to give sanitized data for conversion. Customer should be asked to net off the pending Credit Notes, Debit Notes and Advances against Invoices in both receivables and payables systems before providing the data for conversion into ERP Application. Similarly, the inactive purchase orders can be cancelled, partially received purchased orders can be either received in full or remaining receipts cancelled, and any pending disputes should be addressed before the data comes into ERP System.

The list goes on...

This internal due diligence helps to identify wastes even before data comes into the ERP application.

Another area of waste reduction relates to configuration. By optimally considering the various configuration items, waste can be avoided in the future. For example, in one of my implementations, we identified over 80000 cost components for an item which was adding only 0.5% of the total item costs. Once we removed these components, the costing program which used to take more than 36 hours to complete, finished in just 30 minutes!

2.   *Design high class naming conventions:* Having a well designed naming convention, is the second best design consideration (first being accurate data conversion) values add that a consultant can bring into an ERP Implementation. When it comes to naming conventions, the more the better. If the naming conventions are automated, even better. When it comes to naming conventions try using numeric rather than alphanumeric values where possible. Numeric values support indexation better. Naming convention also help reduce data duplication, especially when it comes to Supplier and Customer Names (which are descriptive in nature). In these data, some of the considerations include, how to handle different vendors with same name (for example, John Smith is a very common name, I think), a convention to use, for example 'Ltd. (Ltd with a dot)' to specify 'Limited'. Naming conventions are simple but powerful tools to ensure long-term optimization of data. Naming convention can also improve system performance, for example numeric data indexes better and retrieves faster than non-numeric data. That is the reason that many of the standard application data has numeric codes as the primary key.

3.   *Design to reduce data duplication:* ERP, by its very design, is an integrated application and the chance of multiple versions of same data existing in the application is remote. However, a smart consultant can still identify potential opportunities to avoid data duplication. For instance, we can reduce data duplication when designing interfaces to ERP from third party applications. Most of the time, all the data that is lying in the legacy application is uploaded and updated in ERP through the interfaces. The attempt is to make ERP the 'Single Source of Data'. While this is a laudable objective, sometimes, it is better to leave the data details in the legacy while bringing in the summary data into the ERP Application. Especially if the legacy system will continue to be used in future.

Unfortunately, we extend the same principle to the data entered into the system through custom, bolt-on solutions. These are customizations developed in the ERP Application for handling specific customer processes. The data lies within the same application database, normally in a 'Custom Schema'. But, we still bring the detailed data into the base application database (what is technically known as 'Apps Schema'). This is a redundant data duplication that the ERP Consultant is building into the system. This need to be avoided.   .

4.   *Design to reduce manual transactions:* While there is a complaint that 'After ERP has come, we are spending more time in data entry', the fact is that almost all ERP Applications has the facility to reduce data entry thereby saving energy, time and money for the organization. For example, you can use EDI to transfer documents to the supplier and customers, you can use automatic bank reconciliation to reconcile your bank statements with the ERP Transactions, use Automatic payments through bank transfers to the vendors, electronically pay salaries to the employees, and use the 'Payment Manager' responsibility to effectively automate your payment processes. The list is endless...

The funny thing is that during ERP implementation, some of the above automation is handled in the application but others are not. Some departments are more application savvy whereas some others are less so. Why does this happen? I think there are three reasons to the above. Primary one is the knowledge of the consultant relating to the above features. A knowledgeable consultant will explain various automation features of the application and work effectively with the customer in implementing these features. If the consultant do not know the automation, he will not mention these features to the customer during discussions and hope that the customer do not come to know. For example, if the consultant does not know how to configure automatic bank reconciliation, he will not even mention that this facility is available in ERP. The second reason is the knowledge and experience of the customer user. Sometimes a demanding customer user can get all the automation that he wants while a passive customer user will live with whatever the consultant offers. Finally, there is a need for automation due to the sheer volume of data. For example, the Employee salary payments are high in volume and need significant level of accuracy. This means that they cannot be handled manually.

Whatever is the reason, a smart consultant can bring in intelligent design in ensuring that manual transactions are reduced so that the labour can be gainfully employed and the data is more accurate.

5.   *Reduce Excessive usage of Paper:* In my opinion, creating a 'Paperless' office should be an important priority for any ERP Implementation. Since the data permanently reside in the database, there is no reason why paper trail is to be kept for audit purposes. For example, despite the fact that both PO and GRN (or MRN – Material Receipt Note) is already available in ERP system, many organizations still insist that physical copies of these documents be attached to the Supplier invoice before making payments to the vendors. I think there are two reasons for demanding physical documents. One is cultural. Going from the safety of physical documents to the uncertain world of 'Paperless' office is traumatic for many finance managers. In addition, the auditing community also do not have tech savvy professionals who can understand the data flow in ERP and hence they insist on paper trail.

While this is not a design issue, ERP Consultant can play a   role in educating the Finance Managers of the features in the ERP application so that they become comfortable with the features of ERP and they, in turn, will start embracing 'Paperless' office.

6. Design to reduce waste of manual labour: One of the key drivers for physical flow of paper in the organization is the requirement for approvals. Physical documents have to be approved by approval authority before the process can proceed. By the use of electronic notifications and exception reporting and digital signature, this requirement can be totally avoided in any organization. The potential is only limited by the knowledge of the consultant.

7. Design to reduce wastes related to bad Account Payable Practices: ERP provided reams of information relating to the pending transactions against each Vendor. It only needs a clear documented process in the organization to ensure that Vendor cash payments will be made only after netting off the existing credit notes and advances. This simple measure can lead to reduction in cash outflow to the organization.

8. Automate to reduce customer disputes: By helping to automate the flow of documents and the associated transactions, ERP help improve customer relationship. Organizations can use EDI to send quotes and invoices to the customer and receive confirmations from the customer. Automatic bank transfers will help automate the receipt, automatic bank reconciliation will help in reconciliation, automatic application will help in applying the receipts to the invoices. All these will help in traceability within the organization as well as reduce disputes with the customer. This also reduces manual labour which can be gainfully employed elsewhere in the organization.

9.   *Schedule batch processes where possible:* Oracle applications provide you with a flexibility to schedule the batch process and run the same at a time when system load is low. There are three factors to consider in scheduling vis. compatibility, frequency and time. If there are compatible programs where the output of one is input to another, you have to design compatibility relationship between these programs so that they run in sequence. However, non-compatible programs can be run in parallel. It is also important to identify and design the best frequency to run the programs. For example, scheduling by 30 minutes frequency as against 15 minutes will potentially double your system performance!. Finally, as relates to timing, best time to schedule some of the programs is when system load is lower like midnight, lunch time etc.

Unfortunately, this is an area mostly ignored during the implementation. But this is one of the key to long-term system performance and by increasing the system speed, will reduce the time taken by the users to enter and complete their transactions. By identifying dependencies and correctly and efficiently scheduling the batch processes, most of the tedious, regular activities can be moved to the time when system load is lower.

10. *Design Exception based reporting:* I can't stress the importance of this more. This is the most ignored aspect in ERP Implementation. The reason is again related to lack of focus during the implementation. Considering that identifying exceptions is one of the most time consuming activities (and hence a waste) post ERP Implementation, it is all the more reason that proper focus is given to this aspect during the ERP Implementation. As everything else related to ERP Implementation, this activity also should be driven by ERP Consultant.
Exception based reporting in not just applicable to reports. A well designed system of alerts, notifications, emails and reports can help in effectively implementing exception based reporting in the system.

11. *Encourage workarounds and process changes to creation of customizations:* Early in my ERP Career, I used to work in an ERP Product named Scala. While this was a good application, there was limitation that this application could not be customized. The upshot was that we were forced think through the requirements of the customer and were forced to come out with innovative workarounds within the application itself. If workarounds were not available, the customer had to change his process to meet with the requirements of the application.

One of the major grouses that I have with leading applications is that they allow too much of customization. The ERP Vendor justifies this by saying that this gives flexibility to the customer. The implementer wants customization since this is where he derives most of his margins. The functional consultant likes customization since it helps him transfer his responsibility to the technical consultant. The customer gets the ego satisfaction that his processes are so unique that even the 'Great' ERP Applications cannot handle his requirement.

Everyone is happy...

Customizations developed without proper analysis will lead to drag on system resources, become a bottleneck during future upgrades and will add to unnecessary control requirements. As mentioned earlier, a poorly designed customization will also lead to data duplication in the system.
Everyone loses in the end...

12. *Encourage use of Standard Reports:* One area where ERP brings in 'Global Best Practices' is in area of standard reports. There are many valuable standard reports in the ERP System. However, none of them are used and Organization ends up in developing custom reports to handle all its report requirements. This is where the gap between 'Global Best Practices' and 'ERP has not brought any Process Benefits to us' happen. And also creation of custom reports, where standard reports are available, will lead to 'Report Duplication', errors, system performance issues and general disaffection with the ERP System.

13. *Effective design of Organizational Structure:* All the ERP packages allow the configuration of the organizational structure. I have seen a few implementations where the Org. structure is either over configured (Too many Operating Units and Warehouses) or under configured. While too many Organizations will make data entry, configuration and Knowledge transfer a nightmare, too few of the organizations can lead to non-availability of effective analytical information.

14. *Encourage the discovery of useful ERP features:* Traditionally an ERP implementation starts off with bare minimum features available in the ERP package. However, the full benefit of ERP package can be attained only if the organization starts using more and more features available in ERP. The most basic and easy to adopt benefit is to use some of the standard reports available in each application. However, once the ERP operations stabilizes, the organization do not show the curiosity to review the available standard reports and incorporate more and more standard reports as a part of the decision making. A few simple examples are the 'Top 10 Customer report' or the 'Top 10 Supplier List', 'ABC Analysis reports' etc. Since most of these reports are parameterized, it will take some experimentation for the organization to identify the correct parameters set to be used to obtain the information relevant and appropriate to the organization.

In the next section, I want to illustrate the practical aspects of these design considerations by taking the design of a single module, in this case, the General Ledger Module in Oracle Applications.

Illustration: Points to consider while implementing General Ledger

I want to illustrate the implementation of the design considerations pointed out above by focussing on the design of General Ledger Module. The following configuration considerations in GL will help in bringing 'Lean'

1. The philosophy of 'Thin GL': In the pre-ERP days, the organizations are accustomed to collecting all the analytical information from the Books of accounts (GL). This includes mostly Customer Balances, Supplier Balances and Assets Details. However ERPs bring in a powerful tool in the form of Subledgers from where Organizations can get almost all the detailed information from the corresponding Subledgers. This means that only a summary information need to flow to GL. This reduces the duplication of information (both in subledger and GL) leading to a 'Thin GL' and more lean accounts operations.

2. Too many or too few Accounting Dimensions: Associated to the above point is the design of Chart of Accounts. Since most of the ERPs offer wide flexibility in design of flexfields / dimensions, many organizations are prone to design more dimensions than necessary. Too many dimensions lead to the following wastes.

a.   Duplication of information between subledger and GL
b.   Waste of time in data entry
c.   Waste of time in error identification and rectification
d.   Waste of precious hardware space
e.   Complexity in GL reporting.

3. Too many GL Journal Entries: In the philosophy of 'Thin GL', almost all the operational accounting entries in GL should flow from the subledgers. Only the period end reversible adjustment journals should be entered in GL. However many organizations use ERP as a huge accounting package and enter far too many accounting transactions directly in GL. This leads to the following wastes.

a.   Waste of time in entering GL transactions.
b.   Waste of time in manually identifying the linkage between these transactions and subledgers

c.   Waste of ERP capability in the subledger modules
d.   Waste associated with generating new reports
e.   Waste associated with manual reconciliation.

4.   *Too many customized reports:* In GL, the report generating tool is very flexible in generating financial reports like P&L, Balance Sheet and CFS. However, many organizations prefer to use custom reports for reporting purposes. This leads to the following wastes

a.   Waste of energy and time in designing and developing custom reports
b.   Waste of energy and time in redesigning custom reports in case of application / database upgrades
c.   Possibility of erroneous data in custom reports.

5.   *Other wastes:* One of the wastes relate to improper design. In this waste the key aspect relate to not incorporating realistic future considerations in the application design. For example, what is the expected life of this ERP application before business is expected to change leading to reconfiguration of this application. A practical example of this was in one of my implementations where the organization told me that they plan to use this ERP application for 15 (!) years and hence we increased the lengths of all the account dimensions to incorporate scalability. The result was a sub-optimal COA design.

Conclusion

The sad reality is that in their quest to implement ERP as a commodity, the consultants and the consulting organization focus on the customer requirement and provides the same to them through ERP. Ideally the focus should be on business issues and problems. Only by solving these will the customer get return on his ERP investment. However, since ERP is considered a commodity, the focus is on costs. To reduce the costs, the organizations (both the implementer and customer) focus on low cost, low maturity and low skilled resources, with one or two senior resources thrown in as a symbol of expertise. Under all these constraints, implementing Lean is a far cry. They (the consultants) do not pause to ask the customer some key questions relating to Business Strategy, Scalability, Application Life, and Key current pain points etc. These are the kind of questions the answers of which will lead to actionable insights on removing long term potential wastes which, in turn, lead to value add for the customer.

What are the process improvements that an ERP consultant can implement to reduce waste and bring in 'Lean' in an organization? What have you implemented in your implementations? Do you approach your ERP Implementation with 'Lean' in mind? Do you factor in 'Lean' in your Design? I am keen to know.

Towards Global Chart of Accounts (Global CoA)

Introduction

While the idea of setting up global chart of accounts (CoA) looks like a beneficial objective, many a times it remains at the stage of wishful thinking. Organizations undertaking this task often find themselves faced with obstacles and tend give up in the early stages of this exercise. The primary obstacle is the multifarious accounting conventions and taxation considerations in the various countries that they do business in.

However, those organizations which persevere with this exercise and complete it reap rich rewards. The most obvious benefit is the vastly expanded knowledge it provides to the organization about its processes. Companies often are surprised to find many common processes that were till then considered 'country specific'. This knowledge helps them to efficiently integrate and standardize processes across the geographies. Another benefit is that this exercise helps them rationalize their country specific processes. Some of the country specific regulations have become out dated and so have those country specific custom processes designed to meet these regulatory requirements. For instance, as India moves to a uniform GST, most of the India specific localization that were catering to the India taxation regime will need to be removed, rewritten or re-looked into. In this case for example, the separate GL nominal accounts created for meeting India specific processes become redundant as the Indian Taxation Regime smoothly integrates into the global taxation practices.

In the light of the above, this article attempts to provide a set of guidelines to the implementation team as they move towards designing a global chart of accounts. It starts by analysing the changing global business landscape that makes global CoA a necessity. Next it identifies the common road blocks in the path to creating a Global Chart of Accounts and lists down the benefits and drawbacks of a global CoA. The article concludes by providing a set of implementation considerations that could help the organizations as they decide to go through with this exercise.

Changes in Business Landscape

Over the last 20 years or so, the global business landscape has undergone changes. These have been catalyzed by global economic growth, the advent of technology that has eliminated the distance between countries and made 24*7 operations a normal scenario and commoditization of ERP to name a few. Given below is a list of the changes to the business global landscape that necessitates the introduction of 'Global Chart of Accounts' (Global CoA).

Globalization and Integration: As globalization and the concomitant business integration marches on, the multinational organizations are faced with new and complex business processes and corresponding accounting challenges. For example, it is almost normal for an Indian company having operations in China, procuring its supplies from Germany and consolidating its payables in Indian Rupee. Here the challenges to payable accounting, inventory valuation and treasury management brings in complexities related to accounting conventions followed in different countries.

Shared services becoming a norm rather than exception: As the global distances gets shorter, it has become a normal practice for organizations to pool and manage their operations like payables and receivables management from a shared service centre located in a low cost country that has the requisite skill sets. Usually a single team in this country handles the operations of units located in different countries. In this situation, having multiple CoAs for different country operation could become a serious bottleneck.

Maturity of ERP Implementations: Over the last ten years or so, ERP has evolved as a major catalyst for organizations to standardize their processes. ERP has enabled the organizations to bring out standard processes across their business units. In some cases it is the lack of flexibility in ERP that has driven the standardization. While the process have standardized in most cases, the nature of accounting those processes is yet to catch up.

Dependence on WEB - Need for a single internal view of the organization: While there are many benefits of Internet, the less talked about is the single view it has brought to the organization about its business. In the pre web period, the HQ of an organization has to wait a month to receive a few handpicked reports from its different international units to get a picture of the health of the organization. The advent of web has changed all that. Now the CFO sitting in Mumbai can receive real time reports of his Chinese, US and German operations on his laptop at the click of a mouse!!. In this scenario, it makes sense for the organization to have a single Global CoA for the CFO to make sense of those multifarious reports.

Increase in quantity and quality of Mergers and Acquisitions (M&A): The major challenge in M&A exercise is process standardization by combining the best practices followed by the two organizations. Many a times they find difference in the way they account similar transactions. One of the ways in which they try to bring about integration is by using common ERP systems. As discussed previously, a common ERP provides optimal results through process and accounting standardization.

New category of accounts created by ERP - Contra Accounts / Intercompany accounts / Cash Clearing accounts etc: This is one instance where ERP and not the business is the key reason for demanding Global CoA. Firms implementing ERP are exposed to a new group of accounts which are not available in their existing CoA. ERP expects these Contra accounts to be set up for all the implementing units. In many cases these accounts could hold significant balances and will require close monitoring and control. As most of these accounts are balance sheet account, their impact will not be immediately felt in the P&L focused analysis. Creation of these accounts is another reason for organizations to go for Global CoA.

However, be careful with Global CoA

While Global CoA is definitely a worthy objective, it is not very easy to achieve. In many cases organizations would already have spent considerable amount of organizational time and resources in designing the present structure. Since the current CoA is designed with organizational requirement in mind, it is better to tread with caution while moving over to Global CoA. The consultant should take pains to understand the detailed design considerations behind the current CoA. She should put in place a stakeholder expectation management strategy while embarking on this exercise. All the stakeholders including Users, Management, External Auditors, Board and the Shareholders are comfortable with the present method of financial accounting and might not want to upset the apple cart.

The strongest argument in favour of Global CoA is the change in global business landscape discussed earlier. It is possible that sooner rather than later, the organization will need to react to the changes. As they say 'it is better to prepare and prevent rather than repent and repair'.

Another argument is the creation of new set of contra accounts to meet ERP requirements and the concomitant control requirements.

Some of the arguments in favour of maintaining the status quo are as follows.

Customization in the current design: If the current system consists of complex customizations a number of inbound and outbound interfaces that transfer data into and out of the existing system, the implementation of Global CoA will call for a detailed review of the accounting impact all these custom programs and interfaces. Since ERP Implementation is a trigger of implementing Global CoA, this will be a beneficial exercise since it helps to evaluate each customization. Global CoA might call for modifying these customizations.

Consolidation requirements: Firms using third party applications like Hyperion for consolidation will need to rewrite a number of account mapping rules prior to using Global CoA. Consultant will have to redesign these rules and get management sign off before commencing the process of implementing Global CoA.

Sensitivity of data: Since the financial data is very sensitive to the organization, there will be a fear that the introduction of the new CoA could bring in increased number of accounting errors and finally could affect the financial reporting. Often this argument is proffered by a senior member of the organization who has been a part of failed ERP implementation in the past. The way to handle this is to do a thorough planning and design a pilot / prototype and get an organizational sign off.

Local Exceptions: If the organization has operations in different countries with different statutory requirements, it could have an impact on the Global CoA. This requirement calls for creation of a set of country specific nominal accounts to handle the different tax regimes and hence may not be amenable to Global CoA. The challenge is to integrate the local tax accounts to the Global CoA.

However, the plus side is that as discussed earlier, the introduction of Global CoA provides an opportunity for the organizations review their country specific taxation processes. Many a time, they are able to rationalize the localization processes and reports thereby reaping scale advantage.

Intensity of training requirements: One of the key challenges in bringing out Global CoA is the intensity of training involved in rolling out the CoA across multiple units. This is all the more daunting if different units had different coding conventions in the past. For example the Hungary Operations may have their asset codes starting with 1, the Owner's equity starting with 2 and Liability starting with 3. However the UK unit will have a convention where liability accounts start with 1, assets start with 2 and revenue starting with 3. It is a serious training challenges to make all these units get accustomed to the Global CoA.

Different accounting conventions followed: This is another case where the difference in accounting conventions calls for different nominal accounts. Typical example is the way different countries handle inventory accounting. While ERP directly debits the asset account on purchase receipt, many countries requires the organization to debit the Profit and Loss account at the time of transaction and reflect the Balance Sheet impact at the period end.

Design Considerations

ERP implementation can act as a catalyst in the organization's move to Global CoA. As a part of the ERP implementation the organization undertakes a detailed analysis to understand the process fit to ERP. This is the ideal time to initiate the process of Global CoA. For one, the organization is ready for a change. Additionally, there are a number of features in ERP which makes it easy to transition to Global CoA. Some of the points which facilitate a Global CoA during ERP implementation are as follows.

Additional best of breed features in ERP: There are various features in ERP which can make your transition to Global CoA necessary as well as smooth. One such feature in Oracle Applications is the concept of Set of books. As the name suggests the SOB can handle multiple books. This feature allows you to use the single CoA across multiple instances / implementation. This is a strong argument for a Global CoA.

Parent Child Hierarchy: Another feature is the concept of parent child hierarchy for reporting purposes. Most of the ERPs allow you to group your child accounts under different parent groups for reporting purposes. Since each child can be grouped under different parents for different reports, you need to use only one CoA for most of your reporting purposes. Of course, your parent child hierarchy will need effective design and constant monitoring.

Flexibility & scalability: It is a good idea to define a superset of the accounts in your organization which will include the normal account codes as well as country specific account codes. Having decided this, use the security rules provided in the package to ensure access control ensure the relevant user - account matrix. This will ensure each user group accesses only the account codes relevant to their unit. This control is required from the statutory requirements such as SOX. Such security features are common for most of the ERPs.

One of the key considerations is scalability and upward compatibility. Ensure that the length of the account code is designed to handle future requirements. For example a 4 digit code, limits to your account number to a maximum of 9999. This may not meet the design criteria of scalability. Normally it is preferable to have 6 digits for an account number.

Additionally ensure to provide sufficient enough gaps between various groups so that additional account numbers can be inserted into the account group in future. For example, if, at present, your fixed asset account numbers are 666101 to 660120 (20 Nominals), you could start the current asset codes from 660151. This leaves 30 nominals for future purposes.

Another aspect of scalability relates to the future growth plans of the organization. If the organization is planning an inorganic growth strategy, the CoA should have the scale to handle the future M&A activities and the incorporation of the new companies into the existing CoA.

Create a team of CoA Ambassadors: As discussed previously, the process of changing CoA is very sensitive and is fraught with many an obstacle. It is very important to have a team of CoA Champions from the customer organization who can own and implement the solution across organization. Their primary role will include coordinating the design of Global CoA, Concept Selling, providing execution support to the rollout of

Global CoA, planning the transition plan, coordinating the security, access and consolidation activities and finally to 'soothe the nerves' at different levels of organization.

Direct from the top: From the perspective of Finance department, this could be the most important initiative which can impact the future finance road map of the organization. It is very important that this initiative be owned and supported at the CFO level. This is not a transactional initiative. Through Global CoA you are attempting to integrate the finance processes and reports and it is imperative that this exercise be directed from top level in the organization.

Benefits

1. 'One View' of organization
2. Easy MIS reporting : Quick and easily understandable reporting
3. Quick consolidation - No fancy account mapping rules required.
4. Better management control throughout the life cycle of the chart of accounts
5. Process standardization should follow from CoA standardization.

Drawbacks

Excessive standardization: This could lead to lowering of the depth and breadth of the country specific data.

Some of the taxation accounts are Balance Sheet accounts and hence are not as closely monitored as P&L Accounts. Chance of surprises could not be underestimated.

Need for close monitoring and tracking. The use / misuse of the new accounting codes due to unfamiliarity in the early phase of implementation calls for intensive training and hand holding in the initial stages and an extended, process driven monitoring and tracking for a significant period of time.

Conclusion

As the organization prepare for ERP implementation, it is a beneficial exercise to conduct a detailed review of the current chart of accounts. The review should include environmental analysis focusing on your industry trends, the industry future direction and your company's current position and the aspired position in your industry. The other aspects to be considered include the current CoA dimensions and the future MIS requirements. The whole exercise is to be considered as a sub project within the scope of the ERP implementation and need to be handled by a team of domain specialists with support from the ERP consultants.

This exercise, if properly done, can reap rich dividend for the organization including a clear understanding of the future road map of the organization, thorough knowledge of the current accounting principles, processes, policies and standards (3PS) and lead to rationalization of these. The end result is a tightly knit organization flexible enough to handle local accounting exceptions.

Design Considerations in Set of Books

There are some critical issues when designing a set of books in a multi OU scenario especially if the OUs operate in the same country.

For example, let us say that you want to create 4 OUs for the Indian Operations. Since the Chart of accounts, Calendar and Currency are the same, the standard procedure is to create a single set of books and link it to each of the OUs differentiating the OUs through the value of 'Company' segment in the chart of accounts.

However the above approach has two associated issues. The first issue is related to the period closing. While each OU tracks their receivables and payables separately, they would like to close the sub ledger periods once their transactions are completed. However this cannot be done in the above scenario since OUs are linked to the same set of books and closing the period in one OU will prevent other OUs from transacting further in the above set of books.

The implication is that in the above scenario, you can close the period only if you complete the transactions in all the OUs. This may not be acceptable to the customer.

Another issue is related to the 'Document Sequencing'. Since the document sequencing is set up at the SOB level, you cannot design different document sequencing rules for different OUs. In this scenario, for example, Payables Invoice No 10002 will pertain to OU1, 10003 to OU2 etc. This has audit and control issues and normally auditors object to this solution.

How do we handle this situation?

The solution is to have separate Set of Books for each of the above OUs and get the financial reports from a consolidated set of books which consolidates data from each of the above set of books. Though it appears complex, this is in reality a very simple solution from mapping point of view.

However there are some problems associated with this solution. First of all, this is counter intuitive. This approach is equivalent to the OUs maintaining their independent books and hence goes against the concept of 'set' of books. In addition, you have to do period closing for multiple set of books and also for the consolidated set of books. Since the consolidated set of books is not the responsibility of any OU, it might get neglected.

Another related issue is the intense knowledge transfer required in the above scenario. There should be a clear

KT processes in place to educate the user in charge of running the consolidation process.

Design Considerations for item coding

Introduction

Intelligent coding of inventory items is one of the most important activities in an ERP implementation for manufacturing organizations. As they approach ERP, the organizations find that their inventory items have been wrongly coded or not coded at all. In addition, they also identify access control issues related to creation of new items. These problems are mostly observed relating to Raw Material and Consumable item rather than finished product items. In addition they also find that the same items have been classified differently for different requirements.

The above issues lead to consequences including lack of control on the inventory items, wrong valuation of inventory, item duplication, wrong / mutually exclusive classification, organization receiving wrong picture of their inventory, lack of real time accurate inventory data etc. Most of these consequences play havoc with the downstream activities including production planning, inventory planning, MRP, available to promise, issues with tax authority etc to name a few.

The main advantage of ERP implementation, if properly done, is that it forces the organization to take a long and hard look at the way the inventory items enter, move through and move out of the organization leading to manifold benefits for all the stake holders in the organization.

Objective of this document

This document aims to provide the ERP Consultant with a set of design considerations and check points to ensure an optimal inventory coding for the purpose of ERP implementation.

Design considerations in inventory coding

Landscape analysis: Before undertaking the exercise, it is beneficial to look at the organization / project landscape. The key points include, the number of ERPs being used in the organization and the commonality of inventory items being used by these packages, the inventory coding constraints imposed by different ERP packages, the inventory reports provided by different ERP packages, the number of external applications presently available in the organization, the flow of inventory data between these applications and the corresponding constraints. Also consider the future ERP roadmap of the organization (are they planning any new ERP implementation for example) and the expected customization requirements.

Ensure that you are only a facilitator: At the outset it must be made clear to the organization that you are going to act as a facilitator in helping the organization to decide on the item coding. It is very important to set this expectation right at the beginning since there is a possibility that the organization may expect you to execute the inventory coding for them. However as a consultant, you may not have a clear picture of the inventory related activities / transactions in the organization. Any coding of inventory without a clear picture of the above will lead to a sub-optimal coding.

Start early: As discussed in the introduction to this article, there are substantial issues related to inventory coding in most of the organizations. Along with this, different part of the inventory are owned by different set of stake holders who have their own internal coding conventions. Added to this, if you have complex coding conventions and large item master it spells a potentially risky situation from the implementation timeline point of view. Hence it is better to sensitize the organization of the importance of inventory coding as early as the project boot camp and follow up the progress in all the senior management meetings.

Involve senior management from the beginning: There is a tendency in the organization to leave the responsibility of item coding to the middle management personnel in the materials management department. Even though they are the drivers of the whole exercise, they may not have the authority to demand output from the line departments. It is very much necessary that top management is involved in this exercise from day one to ensure success of the implementation. If possible, consider inventory coding as a sub project in the exercise of ERP implementation. The consultant must remember that while inventory coding is not a component of the standard ERP implementation plan, this is a critical activity which can derail the project schedules

Involve Finance Department: In many organizations there is a tendency to look at inventory coding as a 'materials management' activity. However finance department is the key user of most of the granular reports related to inventory and consumption. Inventory is one of the key components of 'current assets' in many organization and accurate valuation of inventory has balance sheet and P&L implications. Finance department need to be extensively consulted before the commencement of the coding exercise. They should also be one of the agencies signing off on any deliverable related to the inventory coding program.

Start with the reports: As a first step towards the inventory coding, a consultant need to take a look at the various management reports being used by the organization. There are multiple reports that the top management requires to assess the financial health of the organization. These include Stock Quantity Ledger, Stock Transaction report, ABC Analysis Report, Stock Valuation report, Raw Material / Consumables Consumption report, Cost Sheet etc. A consultant need to be familiar with these reports especially the granularity of reporting, and the categorization of the data required in these reports. Some of the common categories include item type (RM, SFM, FG etc), purchase category (Local / Imported) etc.

What are the details required for querying the item?: Suppose the item required is 'Raw material item, diameter of 0.5 inch, used for customer 1, Imported, purchased from supplier 1 and used for a specific category of FG'. Here each of the details (known as segments in certain ERP product terminology) required to be captured for an item.

What are the details required to be captured in the inventory code?: In database terminology this process is known as normalization. Analyse the data in step 3 and decide which of them need to be captured in the inventory code and which of the details can be captured as attributes to the item. This calls for a detailed knowledge of the product and its features. In the above example, you may have to capture the value of Raw material segment, diameter segment and a unique 3-4 character running serial number need to be captured in the item code where as the other details could be moved to the attributes.

How many segments do the product allow?: Packages like Oracle allows multiple segments to be used in inventory coding. In the above example you can use segment 1 for item type (RM, FG, SFM etc), Segment 2 for diameter (0.25 inch, 0.5 inch etc) and segment 3 can be used for the running serial number. The advantage of this segmentation is that you can set default rules as well as validation rules to ensure that wrong combinations are used. This is not the normal practice of inventory coding and hence will call for increased training and communication effort from your side to familiarize the users to this approach. In the above example, an item may look like 'RM-50-001'

However some applications do not allow multiple segmentation. In this case, you have to ensure manual rules to delineate the segments. While this method is intuitive, it will call for superior training to ensure that user errors are kept to a minimum. This is because, in this method it is difficult to set the kind of default validation rules that was set in case of multiple segments. In this method the above item will read as 'RM50001'.

Use numbers instead of alphabets while coding the inventory: This is important especially if you have a large inventory master. Numeric coding will ensure faster data access enabling faster query fetch and report output. This is related to the internal characteristics of most of the databases currently available.

Keep it simple: And finally keep your inventory coding optimal, intuitive and as close as possible to the way in which inventory is presently created in the organization. This will ensure quicker training and widespread acceptability to the ERP implementation.

Conclusion

Along with realistic design of Chart of Accounts, the appropriate coding of inventory items is one of the key parameters which decide on the success of an ERP implementation. Properly coded inventory can reap windfall benefits to the organization in providing accurate real time inventory data to the organization. The potential benefits to the organization include accurate profitability data, increased inventory turnover, quick ratio matching current ratio, increased cash flow and decrease in inventory carrying cost. Moreover inventory optimization helps in de-bottlenecking of the production flow, freeing up additional space and optimum production and capacity planning exercise.

Considering all the expected benefits, it is very important for the organization to devote superior talent, planning and time to the exercise of inventory coding. Following the above guidelines can go a long way in ensuring minimal surprises while undertaking the above exercise.

Effective use of Exception Reporting in ERP implementation

In many of my ERP implementations, I am surprised to see the kind of customizations that I have been asked to incorporate to ensure that the 'User do not make any mistakes'. Simple ones include, 'Ensuring that the Employee code is numeric', 'The customer name is All Caps' etc. The complex ones include 'Ensuring that XYZ user enters the price correctly', 'The ABC user should enter only a particular type of Purchase Order' or that the 'DEF user raises sales order only for Channel customers'. I invariably end up customizing the application to meet the above requirements since standard applications have a limited capability in meeting some of the above requirements.

When I ask the organization why these customizations are required, after much hemming and hawing, the true reason comes out 'We do not trust our employees to be responsible. They will always make mistakes.....'

We are a theory X organization.

What is common to all the above requirements? As I see it, almost all of it tries to prevent user from entering an incorrect data. Most of the time the user enters incorrect data for two reasons. One, he doesn't know that he should enter the data in a particular format

(Using All caps, Numbers etc). This is simply a process documentation/ training issue. Two, she has access to areas where they are not authorized to enter. This is an access control issue.

Or there may be a fundamental problem in the organization that encourages employees to enter wrong data in the system.

One of the very powerful ways to identify the root issues is the use of exception reports. Once the control requirements are identified, these are very simple and logical and easy to design. There are two key benefits to use of exception reports. One, they help identify the root cause. If a user enters wrong data consistently, this may a simple case of giving her a training. And two, they ensure that some of the major issues come out in the open very early so that they can be identified and resolved. They also address the key issue with customizations in that they do not have any impact on future application upgrades.

Given the benefits of exception reporting, why do most organizations not go for that? There are many reasons. One, the implementation consultants themselves are not aware of the utility / benefits of exception reporting. Two, organizations are scared that employees will make mistakes and thereby their control systems will prove to be ineffective. The way to handle this is to have a combination of exception reports and control systems working together. And thirdly, generation of new exception report may be expensive to the organization. Finally, since exception reports are custom based reports, the customer is not able to see them in action at the requirement gathering stage and hence they decide on the customized controls.

I feel that it is the duty of the consultant to educate the customer on the benefits of exception reporting. It is my experience that many of the customers requirements are related to accurate data entry and minimizing errors and in this, the paradigm of exception reports can provide a lot of long term benefits to the organization.

What do you think? Have you 'sold' exception reporting to the customer in your implementations? What were the problems / issues that you faced? What was the result? Is it beneficial?

DATA MIGRATION

Data Migration Strategies in ERP

Introduction

Effective and efficient migration of data is one of the cornerstones for the success or failure of an ERP implementation. Since a number of questions need to be answered and decisions need to be taken before loading the data into the ERP, lot of planning is required before the data is migrated into ERP.

However, in practice this does not happen. Since data migration is the last activity before go live of an ERP implementation, this very important activity is subject to acute time constraint. With the top management demanding the timely roll out of the ERP, planning for data migration is not given the due importance. This results in junk data going into the new ERP system thereby making the whole implementation suboptimal from day one.

The upshot is clogged database tables, reduction in disk space, performance issues, confused users who are entrusted to clean up junk data in the new system (without much familiarity with the product and the processes) leading to the GIGO phenomenon!. It is not long before the stakeholders lose faith in ERP.

Given this context, the article aims to provide a higher level view of the data migration strategy to be followed in an ERP implementation. The article illustrates the points using Oracle Applications as the ERP product owing to the author's familiarity with the product.

Overall considerations

One, start early. Ideally the data migration planning should start immediately after the first pilot demo of the application (CRP 1). Consultant should start working on the data template as a part of the solution design and continually update the template as the design evolves. Since the migration is a technical process (even though the functional consultant is the owner), it makes sense to involve the developer at the beginning of the process.

Two, decide on how to handle partially completed data. For example, there may be open purchase orders against which material is partially received. There may be vendor invoices which has been paid partially. There could be customer invoices that are collected partially. There could be advances paid to the vendor against which material has been received partially. Organization will need to decide on how to migrate these data into ERP.

Three, consider taxation. Local taxation requirements could pose a challenge. For example, in India we have what is known as TDS (Tax Deducted at Source) that is applicable on a Vendor Invoice as well as on Vendor Payments (Detailed article below). Application will automatically create TDS Invoices on Tax Authority as soon as the Vendor Invoices are generated. Since Tax authority is a Vendor, these invoices will be migrated as part of overall migration plan. Allowing the system to create TDS Invoices will lead to duplication. Consultant might decide to 'Switch On' the TDS feature after the data conversion is completed.

Data Migration Strategy

The data migration strategy consists of the following seven steps as shown in the diagram below:

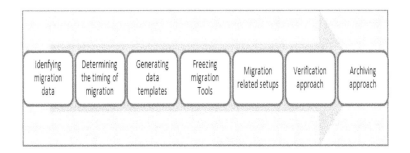

Step 1: The data to be migrated

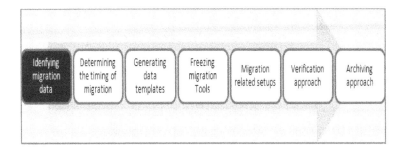

There are four groups of data that has to be migrated during an ERP Implementation. These data need to be entered in the given sequence due to data dependency. The four groups of data are:

Configuration data (Set up data): This group of data determine the general principles and processes to be followed by the ERP system. This is a one-time data entry and is entered manually.

Sub Master Data: These are the set of policies and rules followed in the organization. These include, among others, the payment terms, the delivery terms, the delivery methods etc. This is a one-time entry and entered manually.

Master data: The master data include supplier master, customer master, chart of account master (for each segment), assets master, item master, banks master, currency master, region master, country master, location master, tax master etc. The principle feature of the master data is the extensibility of data. These are transactional data and will need regular updates and maintenance. The mode of data entry will depend on the data volume. Predominantly, different tools are used to load the master data into the application.

Localization requirements form an important part of the master data. It has to be ensured that the templates being used to load master data collects the localization information relating to each master entity.

Since master data is subjected to regular updates, it is prudent to migrate the master data very close to the go live date.

Transaction Data: Completion of transaction data entry is normally called as 'System Go Live'. The transaction data normally consists of the supplier balances, the customer balances, the trial balance, the assets master etc. Since the entry of open balances have financial implications, the above data entry is subject to a series of decisions. The decision include loading open balances versus loading both the open and closed transactions, the archiving requirement, whether to resolve the disputed transactions before or after data migration, whether to post the migrated balances to GL and finally the strategy for validation of data entered into the system. This is a one-time data entry and is normally tool based data load.

Step 2: Timing of data load

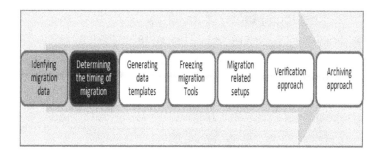

As far as timing of data load is concerned each of the above data follows different time lines. Normally the set up data is completed and signed off before the conference room pilots are completed so that the UAT is conducted in an environment similar to the production environment. Since some of the setup data cannot be modified once it is entered (for example the Accounting Calendar), a lot of care need to be taken before entering the setup data in the system. It is a very good practice to follow a version controlled documentation for the setup data.

Since the sub masters are also one time data entry, these will follow the same process discussed for set up data mentioned above. However, since the sub masters are OU specific, separate data load process need to be used for each OU.

As discussed in the section on data, the master data are subject to continuous updates. Hence the strategy to be followed for master data consists of incremental load as the process moves from CRP1 through UAT. The primary objective of the incremental data entry is to test the completeness of the templates. This means that every load of the master data should be used to test the tools and the templates in addition to the data itself.

The transaction data can also follow the same data load process as the master data. Since the transaction data has accounting implications, it is suggested that every load of transaction data test the whole data load cycle including transferring to GL and validating the accounting entries.

Step 3: Templates to be used

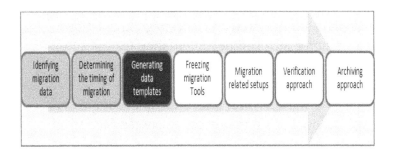

These are sharable components that can be used for data migration of different countries into the regional instance. The template should be designed to handle three sets of data.

The first set of data is mandatory for the database.

These include the primary key values like supplier id, customer id etc. These are unique values.

The second set of the data is required for the effective performance of the application in the organization context. These are organization specific data and could include values like payment terms, delivery terms etc. These are not mandatory for the application to function.

The third set of data is the country specific data. Since the country specific data could be different across countries, the template need to be suitably modified for each country.

As was the case with master data, it is best to freeze the template at the initial phase of the project and test its utility at different phases of the project. This will help in identifying missing data requirements long before the final go live date.

Step 4: Tools to be used

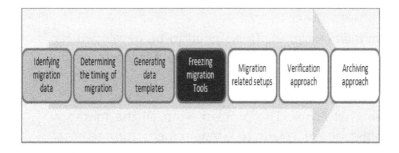

Four different tools can be used to load data into the oracle database. We could use different tools for different types of data.

Desktop Integration: Data Loader can be used as tool which can be used to load data into the oracle tables. Optimally this tool is used in cases where only a single window is used to enter data in case of a manual entry. The tool is easy to use and is very flexible. Some of the data that can be loaded using this tool include chart of accounts, and some of the sub masters. The advantage of this tool is that the consultant do not need technical expertise to load data into the system.

SQL Loader: This tool picks data from a data file in a specific format ('.csv') and loads it into the staging table. From here the data can be moved to the base application tables using SQL Scripts.

Application Standard APIs: These are program interfaces provided by the application vendor to load standard data into the base application tables.

Custom Built Interfaces: These need to be developed for non standard data that need to be loaded into the database

Custom Built Forms: The problem with all the methods described above relate to requirement for technical knowledge. It will be a good idea to spent effort in developing custom built forms to load data into the database. This is similar to the 'Import Manager' tool available in some Applications. The effort spent on this will be well worth since this could act as a component which can be reused across implementations. The development of these forms is a separate project and is not covered within the scope of this document.

Each of these tools needs to be evaluated from the perspective of speed, scope of errors and data volume.

Step 5: Migration related setups

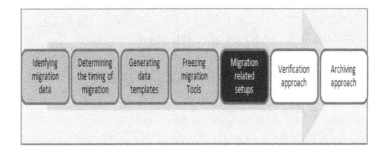

Based on the strategy for data migration, a few setups need to be created specifically related to data migration. These setups can be end dated after the completion of data migration.

Creation of new account codes: A few opening balance intake accounts need to be set up. These accounts get one side of the balance from the sub modules and get the balancing value from the GL trial balance. The accounts include Payables Open Intake Account, Receivables Open Intake account, Assets Open Intake Accounts etc. It should be noted that the creation of the account codes will depend on the migration strategy (specifically whether the transactions taken into the system are going to be posted to GL or not).

Module related Setups: To ensure that the Opening Balance transactions are tracked and closed separately from regular transactions, it is better to create separate identifiers like transaction types, transaction sources etc in different applications. For example in the auto accounting setup in AR in Oracle, you may need to create separate transaction types or standard memo lines for taking in receivables opening balances.

Step 6: Post Migration Verification and signoff

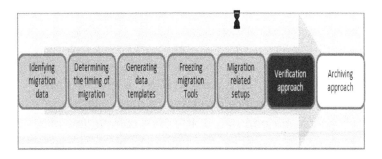

This is the most important step in data migration since this step transfers the ownership of the data to the customer. Each element of data migrated into the application should be documented by the consultant and accepted and signed off by the customer. The aspects to be considered include, for each element, the verification criteria and the supporting documents. It is better to create a separate folders to hold the migration data. The 'Input' folder will be owned by the customer. They will place the validated data in this folder. The consultant will pick this data, load it into the system and upload the 'Output' folder with the uploaded data and the supporting documents. Ideally supporting documents should be the standard application reports. For example, the supporting document for Supplier Master could be the Supplier Listing Report, for Item Opening Balance could be the Inventory Valuation reports and so on.

It is important to have individual super user sign off on each data element and the customer Project Owner signoff on the completion of data migration phase.

Data Archiving

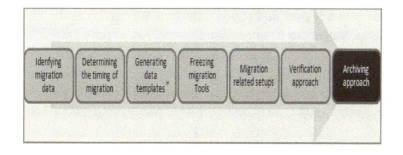

Decision on data archiving is dependent on various factors including the statutory requirements of various countries, reporting requirements and transactional information requirements. For statutory requirements some countries are expected to maintain up to 7 years of data. Also, the organization may want refer to some older data for internal auditing and comparison purposes and finally users may want to refer back to more recent transactions.

Based on each of the above, the archiving period will vary. While statutory reporting may require 7 years of data, comparison reporting may call for 4 to 5 years of data and transactional requirements will call for the last one year's data.

In data archiving, the organization could follow any of the following strategies. The issue of data archiving is applicable to the intake of transactional data discussed earlier.

Do not load any past and closed data into the Applications. Import only opening balances: For AR and AP, import only the current balances in the respective control accounts. For any partially completed transactions, import only the open balances. Close out as many transactions as possible by paying off AP invoices for example. By making the data compact, this method is easier to apply and is intuitive. The major advantage of this method is that the organization can do a data clean up exercise before loading the data to Oracle. However the drawback of the above approach is as follows.

a. Historical transactions will not be available in oracle for statutory requirements: Some countries require 7 years of archived data. This information will not be available in Oracle if the above method is followed. The way to handle this is to either have an archive instance with the historic data or to back up the historic data in an archive databases and have some of the key reports prepared in discoverer pointing to the database.

b. Transactional linkages will not be available: Some of the current transactions may require the user to track back to some older transactions. In the above approach, the past transactional information will not be available

2. Load only the past data corresponding to the current transactions: In this method, load all the transactional data relating to current open balances. For instance, if you have a partially paid invoice, enter the original invoice and the partial payments into Oracle. Most of the time, this takes care of user's requirements discussed above.

3. Load all the data from the legacy system to Oracle: There is no data cleaning in this method. This is more like a data dump from legacy system to Oracle. In addition to increasing the disk requirements, this leads to duplication of data as well as performance issues.

For options 1 and 2, the organization will have to consider an instance strategy for archive instance as a part of the detailed instance strategy. The instance strategy should involve the infrastructure as well as the MIS reporting linkages in addition to the archived data.

Final Outcome

The final output of the Data Migration Strategy discussions is a table as given below. This is a sample list

No	Data Element	Type	Mode of data entry	Tool	Verification document
1	Configuration data	Setup data	Manual	None	Configuration document
2	Payment Terms	Sub-master	Tool based	Data Loader	On Screen
3	Delivery Methods	Sub-master	Manual	None	On Screen
4	Other Sub-masters	Sub-master	C by C	C by C	On Screen
5	Supplier Master	Master	Tool based	SQL Loader	Master Listing Report
6	Customer Master	Master	Tool based	SQL Loader	Master Listing Report
7	Item Master	Master	Tool based	SQL Loader	Master Listing Report
8	Assets Master	Master	Tool based	SQL Loader	Assets Register Report
9	Bank Master	Master	Manual	None	On Screen
10	Country Master	Master	Default	None	Default
11	States Master	Master	Default	None	Default
12	City Master	Master	Default	None	Default
13	Chart of account	Master	Tool based	WEB ADI	CoA Listing report
14	Vendor OB	OB	Tool based	API	Supplier Open Balances report
15	Customer OB	OB	Tool based	API	Customer Open Balances report
16	Assets OB	OB	Tool based	API	Assets Register report
17	Item Quantity OB	OB	Tool based	API	Inventory Valuation report
18	Item Cost OB	OB	Tool based	API	Inventory Valuation report
19	Trial Balance	OB	Tool based	WEB ADI	Trial Balance report

Conclusion

Configuration and Data migration are the two most important activities determining the success of an ERP implementation. An accurately migrated data is a demonstration to the stakeholders that the ERP system is a reflection of their current organization. This increases their confidence in the application and in turn is a key factor in the ultimate success of ERP implementation. In many instances, this important activity does not get the kind of serious attention that it deserves.

By following a well laid out data migration strategy, organizations can ensure an effective and efficient data migration.

.

Intake of Opening Balance

There have been a number of questions on the correct process of taking in Opening Balances in an ERP Implementation. As mentioned in my previous article on Data Migration Strategies, the Opening balances fall into the following items.

(Note: I use the word 'Subledger' and 'Applications' interchangeably. Both refer to applications of original entry like Receivable, Payables, Assets and Inventory)

1. Customer Balances
2. Supplier Balances
3. Assets Balances
4. Inventory Quantity
5. Inventory Cost
6. GL Balances (Trial Balance)

All the items above have accounting implications. The key challenge is that while all the above creates accounting transactions in the respective applications, thus creating balances in GL, intake of GL Trial Balance also creates balances for the same accounts. This doubles the account balances in GL creating a Subledger to GL mismatch.

Different consultants follow different practices to handle the above scenario. The methodology falls into four types.

1. Do not transfer the subledger accounting entries to GL.
2. Transfer the subledger balances to GL, but map the same account to both sides of the subledger accounting entry. This will ensure process integrity while not creating any accounting impact in GL.
3. Transfer the subledger balances to GL and then pass a reverse journal in GL
4. Transfer the subledger balances to GL Configure the system so that the accounting entries are automatically reversed.

While approach number one above should not be used, the approaches two and three have a drawback that GL to Subledger drilldown will not be possible. The best is approach four.

This article explains the steps to be followed in the approach four above.

Step 1: Create four separate OB intake accounts for the four applications. Map these accounts as net off (or set off) accounts for Creditors, Debtors, Assets and Inventory transactions. The OB intake accounts should be Balance sheet accounts. Normally I use the nominal account starting 9. For example 999001 is Creditors OB Intake Account, 999002 is Debtors OB Intake Accounts,

999003 is Assets OB Intake Account and 999004 is Inventory OB Intake account.

Step 2: Map these accounts as the offset accounts in the respective applications.

Step 3: Migrate Opening Balance in respective applications. The accounting entries in the respective subledgers will look as follows.

For Payables OB

999001	Debit
Creditors A/c	Credit

For Receivables OB

Debtors A/c	Debit
999002	Credit

For Assets OB

Fixed Assets A/c	Debit
999003	Credit

For Inventory OB

Inventory A/c	Debit
999004	Credit

Step 4: Post the accounting entries to GL. Since these are the only transactions in GL, Trial Balance will be as follows.

Creditors A/c	Credit
Debtors A/c	Debit
Fixed Assets A/c	Debit
Inventory A/c	Debit
999001	Debit
999002	Credit
999003	Credit
999004	Credit

Step 5: Print the verification reports and get the sign off from respective customer super users for successful migration of the opening balances in their applications.

Step 6: Modify the configurations made in Step 2 and replace the OB Intake accounts with the correct offset accounts in the respective modules.

Step 7: Enter the GL OB (Trial Balance as GL transactions in the same period. You can use web ADI to upload the transactions. When you upload the OB, ensure to replace the Creditors, Debtors, Assets and Inventory accounts with the corresponding OB Intake Accounts. This will be the entries in the OB Intake accounts from the GL Trial Balance

999001	Credit
999002	Debit
999003	Debit
999004	Debit

As you can see, Step 5 creates the opposite side of the accounting entry in the OB Intake Accounts. OB Intake accounts get one side of the accounting entry from the transactions entered in the respective modules , the other side of the accounting entry will come from GL transactions. This means that after posting the GL transactions, these accounts will have a zero balance.

Step 8: Verify that the OB Intake Accounts have zero balance.

Step 9: Disable (or end date) the four OB Intake accounts. (so that people do not enter transactions in these accounts by mistake)

Step 10: Print the Trial Balance and get signoff from finance super user

Step 11: Get signoff from Customer PM for closure of Data Migration Phase.

.

Of course, the above is a broad strategy for data conversion and there may be pitfalls as you execute the process. I have already documented these challenges in the previous article on Data Migration Strategies.

What is the advantage of this method? Ensuring zero balances in OB Intake accounts acts as a control check on the integrity of the migration process. For example, any balance in the intake account will mean that the total balances in the subledger did not tally with the balances in the GL. This means that either subledger figures are wrong or GL figures are wrong - both of which could point to a loophole in the customer's current accounting system.

Another advantage of this approach is the 360 degree tracking. You can go from Subledger transactions to the GL and also drill down from GL to the respective applications and thence to the individual transactions. This smoothens the reconciliation process.

ERP
IMPLEMENTATION

Solution Architecture for ERP Implementation

In the summer of 2007, I had the opportunity to work as the Solution Architect for a global program of a world leading organization with operations across 3 continents.

The customer was in the process of implementing Oracle Applications solution across the entire organization. For each project they had a process of assigning a solution architect whose responsibility was to deliver a Solution Architecture Document.

This organization had a well defined Architecture department with over 400 architects. The team included specialists in the area of applications, information services, security, disaster recovery and operations. The team also included a set of Enterprise architects and a group of Solution architects. While the enterprise architects focused on the overall architecture of the company, Solution architects were specific to each project. Every project started off with a solution architect. Every solution architecture document addressed a specific part of the enterprise architecture document.

I was the solution architect for the project to integrate the Financial Processes into a global single instance.

As per Zachman's model, the architecture of a company can be grouped under the following areas. Contextual, Conceptual, Logical, Physical and Detailed. In each of these areas, the architect need to ask the following 6 communication questions (What, where, when, why, who and How).

For my project I concentrated on the Conceptual, Logical and Physical part of the above 5 architecture areas.

Solution architecture in a typical ERP implementation will address the following.

1. Overall architecture
2. Context
3. Application Architecture
4. Information Architecture
5. Infrastructure architecture
6. Security Architecture
7. Operations and control architecture.

In each of these areas, you start off with a conceptual architecture, which is then detailed into a logical architecture and finally further elaborated into physical architecture. While the conceptual architecture is at a high level, the architecture gets progressively elaborate as we move to the lower levels.

Before I proceed further, I want to address a critical

question. Should the Solution architect be an expert in each of the above areas? It is impossible for one consultant to be an expert in all these areas.

The answer is No. Solution architect need not be an expert in all these areas. She should be an expert in one or two of the areas and should have a clear idea of the business. The role of the Solution Architect is more of a co-ordinator who identifies the key resources / experts in each of the above areas and gets their inputs and consolidates the same into a single Solution Architecture document. Since the role calls for extensive discussion with experts, it is essential for the Solution Architect to have good communication skills.

Overall Architecture

This is like an introduction to the Solution Architecture document and sets the stage for the details that follow. Overall architecture documents the applications (both internal and external), the technologies used, and the overall philosophy of the project. While it should not be very detailed (so as to break the mystery as it were) while it should also give sufficient high level details to spur the interest of the user of the Solution Architecture document.

Context

Every project happens within a context. The context could be either a business context or a technological context. Sometimes the context could be the IT vision of the organization where ERP solution is a part of a broader digital transformation initiative. Most of the time, the context is the high level, near / medium term IT roadmap of the organization. It is very important for the Solution architect to understand, document and validate the context under which the ERP solution is being implemented.

The diagram below shows the context diagram for an ERP Implementation for diary products company in India.

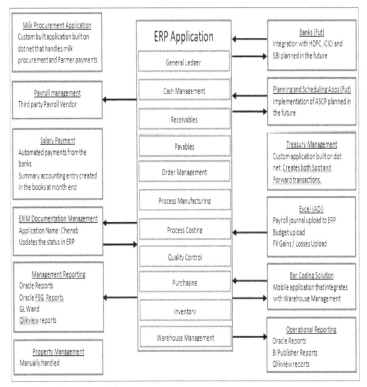

Application Architecture

Normally a Solution Architect considers only the application architecture aspect of the ERP implementation. Almost like a primordial reflex, the solution architect will go around collecting information on various applications that integrate with the ERP system and then prepare a neat diagram with many boxes and arrows showing the various applications and their integrations.

While primarily application architecture does that, it also looks at:

1. *The application landscape*: In this the solution architect identifies the various applications that interacts directly and indirectly with the ERP system. For example, if application A provides inputs to Application B which in turn provides inputs to your ERP system, both applications A and B should be reflected in your application architecture.

2. *Type of integration*: There could be a number of questions that the solution architect should ask when she is looking at under the above heading. Key aspects to be considered include the data flow direction. Is it inbound (data flowing into the ERP system) or outbound (ERP system is providing information to another application).

The application architecture will have a close linkage with the Operations architecture mentioned above when it comes to Batch Program based integration and error detection and tracking.

3. *Other Questions:* The other questions that need to be addressed in Application Architecture are:

1. What is the type of information that flows between different applications.

2. What is the direction of information flow?
3. What is the volume of data flow (normal, peak)
4. What are the workflows and approvals that accompany these information flows?
5. What are the various documents that flow between the applications? Are they maintained in physical form or electronic form?
6. What are the linkages between the various applications? The linkages will include Primary Key, Foreign Key, Field mapping etc
7. Is the information transfer real-time or batch?
8. What is the integration type? Point to point, through middleware, through FTP, or based on Workflows?
9. Will the information transfer be automated or will there be manual intervention
10. How is field mapped between applications?
11. Will the data transfer between source and target application be 1 to many, many to 1 or many to many?
12. What are the control and check points to be considered?
13. What is the reporting process? How will errors be reported?
14. How will the errors be handled?

Given below is a Conceptual Application Architecture Diagram

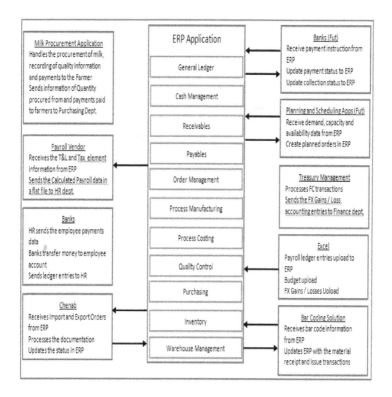

Milk Procurement Application
Handles the procurement of milk, recording of quality information and payments to the Farmer
Sends information of Quantity procured from and payments paid to farmers to Purchasing Dept.

Payroll Vendor
Receives the T&L and Tax element information from ERP
Sends the Calculated Payroll data in a flat file to HR dept.

Banks
HR sends the employee payments data
Banks transfer money to employee account
Sends ledger entries to HR

Chenab
Receives Import and Export Orders from ERP
Processes the documentation
Updates the status in ERP

ERP Application
General Ledger
Cash Management
Receivables
Payables
Order Management
Process Manufacturing
Process Costing
Quality Control
Purchasing
Inventory
Warehouse Management

Banks (Fut)
Receive payment instruction from ERP
Update payment status to ERP
Update collection status to ERP

Planning and Scheduling Apps (Fut)
Receive demand, capacity and availability data from ERP
Create planned orders in ERP

Treasury Management
Processes FC transactions
Sends the FX Gains / Loss accounting entries to Finance dept.

Excel
Payroll ledger entries upload to ERP
Budget upload
FX Gains / Losses Upload

Bar Coding Solution
Receives bar code information from ERP
Updates ERP with the material receipt and Issue transactions

Physical Application Architecture diagram goes into deeper level of the interrelationships between all the applications in the conceptual application architecture diagram

Given below is an example Physical Application Architecture diagram showing the Flows between Oracle Applications and Payroll Vendor for Payroll processing. The Solution Architect will generate detailed Physical Application Architecture diagram to show the various flows between every application similar to one below

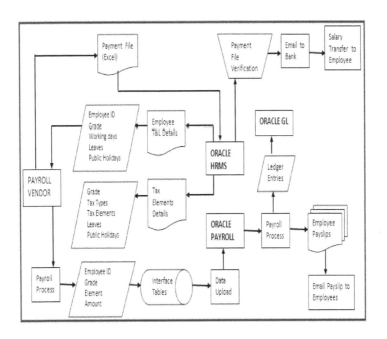

Information Architecture

This closely corresponds to the application architecture. Information architecture deals with the type and volume of information that passes between various applications as well as between different modules in the ERP application.

Conceptual Information Architecture diagram is given below.

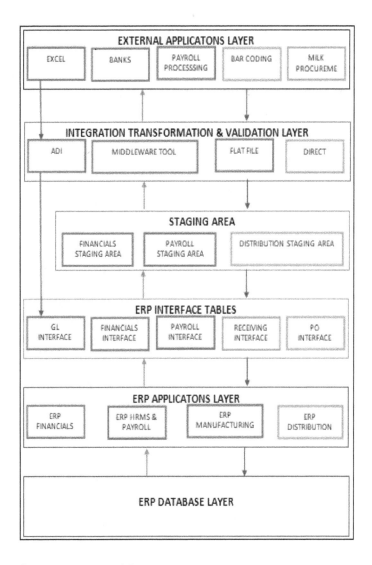

Infrastructure Architecture

Infrastructure architecture should consider the

following. This is a very highly technical aspect of the Solution Architecting and Solution architect will do well to consider these aspects very early in the solution. Also this is an area that undergoes multiple revisions and finally this is the area which, if not done correctly, can lead to performance issues in the future.

1. Hardware sizing: This is normally done by the hardware vendor. However it is very important for the Solution architect to have an idea of the logic used behind the hardware sizing.

2. No of nodes: This is a very important decision. In single node installation a single, parent server takes up all the performance loads while in multi-node installation, multiple nodes share the performance loads. Multiple nodes help in load balancing and performance optimization. However, post go live management is better with single node installations. And finally, the installation complexity is higher with multi-node installations. Most of the time, this is a decision taken as a part of point 1 above.

3. Disaster recovery architecture: One aspect of Infrastructure architecture, esp. in big implementations is related to planning for disaster recovery. Some of the questions are: How will the disaster recovery be handled? What is the location of the DR server? What is the logic of selecting that location? What is the lead time in moving from the main server to the disaster recovery server?

What is the mode of data transfer between main server and DR server? Real time data transfer can be very expensive. Many organization opt for some lag between the data transfers. The number of hours of data lag is very important. For instance, if the data transfer happens every four hours, and the disaster happens after 3.5 hours of the last data transfer, the 3.5 hours of data has to be manually entered in the DR server.

Load balance of disaster recovery server is another critical item. During normal hours, only a part of the server need to be dedicated to ERP and other applications can run on the same, but during the disaster period, many of the other applications will need to close to pave way for more load to be used by the ERP application.

How will the functional users be informed of the disaster and how they will start accessing the DR server? And finally, disaster recovery also should plan for data entry by having buffer resources to enter the data backlog.

4. Moving back to the main server. Part of the disaster recovery architecture should also consider the process of closing the DR server and moving back to the main server once the core issue have been resolved. Since this is a planned activity, it is much less complex. Detailed procedure documentation and approval processes should be maintained during the entire process of moving to the DR server and then moving back again to the main server.

5, *Application performance*: In a 3 tier architecture, the information is entered in a thin client and this gets processed in multiple servers in the background. This could lead to a lot of wait time for the user between the time she enters the data and the system fetches back the process data. For most of these parameters, there are clear international benchmarks which the technical consultants should be aware of.

Security Architecture

Security Architecture is concerned with ensuring the security of the application and the data base. The security architecture for this solution is dependent on the overall security policy and network access policy of the organization.

Typically the security architecture should cover the following aspects.

1. *Data Security*: How will the database security will be maintained? How will the administrator maintain the passwords? How can the database password be protected? What is the policy for granting access to the database.

2. *Application Security*: How will the application be secured? How will the access to the application be controlled? How will the activity in the application be monitored? What kinds of Alerts are required? What are the possible error scenarios? How each scenario will be managed? What is the application security policy?

3. *Access Control*: What is the firewall policy of the organization? What is the network access policy? What is the application access policy? Will single sign-on be used? Will Active Directory be used to manage accesses? How the access to the network be managed from within the country? From abroad? What is the process of IP Management? Will static IP be used? Will dynamic IP be used? Will VPN be used? What is the process of accessing the network? Is logging in to the network mandatory for connecting to the application? Will separate accesses be used for database and application?

4. *Password Policy:* This policy applies to the management of passwords for the network, the database and the application. The key aspect here is the ownership hierarchy. Some of the questions that need to be addressed are: How are passwords going to be managed? Will we have tracking of passwords history? How frequently the passwords will be maintained?

5. *Inactive accounts management*: How will the inactive accounts be identified? Managed?

6. New account creation: What is the new account approval and creation policy? What is the procedure? What is the document tracking?

Operations and control architecture

This part of the solution architecture covers how the standard day-to-day operations on the application will be handled on an ongoing basis once the application goes live. The key questions that need answering are:

1. Back up strategy: What is the frequency of database backup? what is the frequency of application backup? Will it be a cold backup (Application and database are stopped before backup) or a hot backup? What is the tool used to keep the backup? Will the back up be on a CD, on tape or on another drive? How many days of data backups will be maintained? What time of the day the backup will be taken? What is the expected duration for taking the back up? For restoring the applications?

2. Process scheduling strategy: Every application will have a set of batch processes that need to be run during lean periods. So the questions are, What are the key processes to be scheduled? What are the interdependences and sequences? How will they be scheduled? What is the strategy in case of a process failure? What processes will be run during the weekdays? What processes will be run on weekends? On holidays? Who are the owners of the processes?

3. *Performance tracking*: The administrator should regularly track the performance of the system. This aspect of the architecture asks questions like, what are the key parameters to be tracked? How will the admin know that intervention is required? What are the expected issues and expected resolution plans?

Conclusion:

Every project, big or small, need to start with a solution architecture document. Initially the Solution architect will develop the logical architecture and progress to physical architecture as they emerge. In this way, the solution architecture document is an evolving document. While the solution architect should ideally be focusing on the end user (A house is there for people to live, nor for carpenters, plumbers and electricians to produce their deliverables), unfortunately, Solution architecture is considered as a technical activity and hence do not get the due review and importance from the project implementation team.

ERP Journey - 10 Risks faced by an SME

So you are the Owner / CEO / CIO of an SME. You have heard a lot about the benefits of having an ERP in your organization. You have heard that it will bring in data integrity and efficiency to your operations. You can't wait to start..

Wait a sec, have you considered the following risks.

Small enterprises like yours face some typical risks while embarking on your ERP journey. The risk start at the time of evaluating the ERP and could, if not mitigated effectively, potentially go on for years after you have attained that holy grail of all implementations, vis. go live. Let us take a look at the top 10 risks that you may face in your ERP implementation journey.

1. Process Knowledge Risk: While your enthusiasm to go for ERP is appreciable, take a step back and see if you know your business processes. Do you know who are your top 10 customers, do you know how your balance sheet is generated, do you know the various statutory rules that apply to taxation for your industry, do you know the different types of items you purchase, do you know the conceptual / theoretical process of manufacturing key products, do you know how cost is calculated and tracked in your organization

Do you know.....

All right, you are the Owner / CEO / CIO, you are not supposed to know the details of these processes. But the question is does your Organization know these processes. Of course, there are people in your organization who know these processes. The key question is, is there anyone in your organization who know the integrated business processes in your organization? If the answer is yes, then, let me say this, you are very lucky. Get that person to quickly document the business process. If needed, get an expert to sit with him and get your processes documented. If you have documented your processes, you have crossed the first hurdle and mitigated the first risk. There is a good chance that your ERP implementation will be successful.

2. Pain Points Knowledge Risk: Do you know which are your top five, ten pain points? I have seen many organizations deciding to go for ERP implementations only because, either, their headquarters told them to do so, or, because their competitors have gone in for ERP. For them ERP is just another IT application like, say, MS Office, Excel or that tax application your internal auditor uses once a while. They do not have any clear expectations from ERP. They do not have a clear objective when going in for implementing ERP. If you do not know your pain areas, the chances are high that they will not be addressed during the implementation. Know your pain points, and have a clear measurable goal of incrementally reducing the pain points during and after the ERP is implemented.

3. Product Risk: So which product are you going to choose? Oracle? SAP? Any other? A friend of mine, who owns an SME company which implemented ERP, told me that while they were looking out for ERP, they did not have any awareness of any other ERP applications being available (other than SAP and Oracle) out there. This is a typical problem being faced by SMEs. Lack of information about product options means that you run the risk of choosing an application which may not be a fit for your organizations. SME industry being fragmented as it is, there is no single source of learnings related to ERP procurement, lessons learnt etc.

4. Product Versions Risk: So finally you have decided to go for a product. The next risk relates to the product version that you want to procure. As an SME, you will not be able to handle the implications of wrong choices. In percentage terms, a wrong choice could lead to monetary impact for your organization. There will be pressure from those in your organization to go for the latest version. After all that is the product direction and the vendor will be giving you good discounts to buy the latest version (they want 'early adopters'). Please remember that buying ERP is not like buying a consumer durable or a music system. The bigger / the latest may not be the better 'for you'. I think that it makes sense for you to go for a tried and tested version. After all, you are not a Fortune 500 company (at least till now, who know what can happen once ERP is implemented)

5. Consultants Competence risk: As an SME, you may not be able to afford the TCSs and Infys of the world. This means that you have to go with smaller partner organizations. This decision entails its own risk. The smaller organizations may not be able to attract and retain talent. They may not have sufficient number of senior consultants with thorough implementation experience in SME sector. The consultants may not have enough business experience or will not be able to understand your business requirements. Or the consultants may leave midway through your project leaving you high and dry and unable to cope up with the time and cost overruns that entail as the implementation partner searches the market for a new consultant and then the new consultant takes his own time understanding your business process and the status of your implementation.

How do you handle such risk? One way is to modularize your implementation. Divide the project into optimum number of Stop Gates where you can take a 'Go - No Go' decision. Each Gate should have its own documented deliverables. The implementation methodology of most of the big application vendors automatically considers these 'Stop Gates'. If the methodology do not (consider these gates), insist that the implementation partner divide the project into suitable number of manageable milestones ('Stop Gates') with their own deliverables.

6. Internal Knowledge Risk: As an SME, chances are that there are only few resources in your organization possessing an Organization wide process knowledge. While these resources are valuable to you, remember that these resources will be much more valuable to the ERP ecosystem (competitors, Implementation Partners, Product Companies, Consulting Companies) once your implementation is completed. In case you have depended a lot on these resources to drive your implementation, without ensuring that the knowledge is transferred across the organization (building up internal capabilities), you run a serious risk of breakdown once the application / implementation goes live and the resources leave you.

How do you handle such risks? There are many ways to do that. First, as I mentioned before, is detailed documentation of the Business Process, the solution, the configuration, user manual, user training etc. Another way to handle it is to have multiple resources tagged to the main resource. As an SME you may not be able to afford that. Another way to handle this risk is through the use of an expert partner who can provide continuity for your implementation in difficult times.

7. Localization knowledge risk: As an SME your exposure and impact of this exposure to local taxation rules is much more significant than, say, a large enterprise. This means that solution of country / tax localization is a very important aspect of your implementation. The statutory / localization might have three types of implications / impacts in the order of increasing risk and complexity. They are one, reporting impact, two, transaction & reporting impact and three, transaction, accounting and reporting impact. The ERP application should support country localization. If not, the implementation partner should be able to suggest an acceptable solution for country localization. In this case it is very important for you (as the implementing organization) to be aware of the key requirements relating to your localization / statutory reporting. Ability of the application to meet these requirements should be a key criteria in deciding on the application to procure.

8. Period Closing Risk: Other than going live, the main milestone in any ERP implementation is the Closure of the first period. This activity entails many sub activities and is important for external reporting. At the beginning of the project itself you should be aware of how much time you are taking to close the period (both month and year). You should have a clear KPI to reduce this value post implementation. You could say something like 'Currently we close the month on the 10 of the next month and the year by the 20th of February every year. After ERP is implemented I want the month closing to come down to 5 days in the first year, 3 days in the second year and target 'one day closing' from third day onwards'. This will give you a powerful statement of direction for your ERP implementation.

9. Continuous Support / Maintenance Risk: Once you have gone live on ERP, you are bound to face issues, both major and minor, on an ongoing basis while using your ERP application. To resolve this you will require continuous support. No problem, many vendors offer you continuous support (at a fee, of course. In case your vendor do not have a dedicated team to support you post your go live, reject them during the procurement stage itself.

Assuming that your vendor has the necessary support available, the problem doesn't end there. Most of the technical support teams do not understand business, but understand only technology. So to interact with them, you have to be technology savvy. And that is a problem for an SME like you, who would rather invest your time on improving business, rather than learning technology.

How do you handle this? I wish there were easy answers. There are none. If you train some of your staff on technology, they are bound to quit sooner or later. To counter this attrition, you have to continuously have a pool of tech savvy resources. Training your resources on technology is not what you are there for.

You could outsource this aspect of operation. However, it is not very easy to find agencies / organizations that are into such activities. And they come at a price.

10. Lack of support knowledge risk.: In addition to knowledge of technology, you also need to be aware of your sources of support. There are vast sources of support for your problems available in the internet. There is the Vendor's portal, Vendors support portal, Vendor managed user forums, independent user forums, Specific business communities, generic technology communities (like IT Tool Box) and individual consultant blogs (like the one you are reading) available out there which can provide you with the knowledge and support that you require, often free of cost or at a nominal cost.

The problem is again the tech savviness of the organization. If the senior management and the key team are inquisitive, open to learning and open to embracing technology, then you have an advantage in running an efficient and effective ERP application

Product Demo: A great way to introduce your team

Product demo is one of the first activities that the implementation team performs after they reach the customer site for an ERP implementation. In this phase, the customer team becomes aware of the product they are going to be using for years to come. In an Oracle Apps implementation for example, the product demo is done in a demo database called 'Vision Demo Database'. This is a preconfigured database with all the standard flows built in to detail.

In my experience, the implementation team takes this phase very lightly. For them this is a phase where you put in some stop gap consultants and ask the customer to go through the user manuals and acquaint themselves. For the customer also this phase is like a trailer, the boring period of time before the 'real movie' starts.

The implementation team starts the vision demo is by using the existing data and minimally tuning it to the customer's requirements. For example, they may create a supplier named 'Test Supplier' and a few items like 'Test Item' etc. Some of the standard processes are demonstrated in a demo company called 'Vision Operations'. Even those customer users who start the demo very eagerly, quickly lose interest in the proceedings since they are not able to identify with the data!

The end result is that the implementation team has lost out on a fantastic opportunity to gain the confidence of the customer. Since the customer's confidence in the product and on the implementation team is a prerequisite to successful implementation, the 'real' activities of the project will start with the baggage of a 'sceptical' or a 'neutral' customer as against a possible 'convert'.

The best way to use the Vision Demo effectively is to replicate customer's configuration in the Vision instance as much as possible. For example, you could create an Organization as the customer's organization and link their set of books to the organization. Use actual suppliers, actual customers, actual invoices, payments, actual users etc. Most importantly, use actual items and actual warehouses where they will be transacted.

To improve the effectiveness, you could create the financial reports with the customer's chart of accounts and take out the actual financial reports after posting the transactions to GL. Nothing inspires confidence in the project more than seeing your actual financial transactions being recorded correctly. This inspires confidence in the finance team who will be one of the signatories to almost all the deliverables in the project.

Of course there are limitations. 'Vision Instance' is not a localized instance, meaning local taxes are not configured. Prior to starting the demo phase, the Project Manager should check if 'Localized' demo instance is available. Most of the vendors have localized instances.

Also, it will be a good idea to share the data migration templates to collect the customer data for demo instance. This will act as a first check on the quality and completeness of the template as well.

There are many advantages to this approach. The implementation team will be able to appreciate the potential implementation risks very early in the project. In addition, this exercise benefits the implementation team by giving them an early understanding of the customer's business. Same with the customer. They will be able to understand the limitations of their data and become sensitive to potential process changes that may come their way.

However this is not easy. The consultant has to handhold the customer to filling the template for example. Since this process is done very early in the implementation cycle, both consultant and customer are getting used to working with each other and any open communication will be difficult. That is where the data templates will help.

Few of the potential challenges that this exercise can throw up could be Inventory Item Coding, Unit of Measure (UoM) and its conversions and localization related issues. The earlier the consultant becomes aware of these issues, the better it is for the implementation.

Delivering Healthy Projects: My view

Everyone wants to deliver projects which are healthy and adds value to the customer. That is what each consultant wants when she goes to a customer location to implement a project.

The question is, how do you deliver a healthy project? Is there any secret?

I am giving below some of the tricks that I have learned over my short implementation experience.

During my 10 years experience of delivering full cycle ERP Implementations, I have learned that the trick to deliver a good project is to get the customer involved very early in the project.

In the initial part of any project, the load / effort incurred by the implementer is very high. Most of the time, the customer is not involved, is disinterested or is skeptical about the whole process. In addition, there will be situation where the customer user is simply afraid of the purpose of ERP implementation and will not take any active interest.

As the project progresses, the customer team starts taking some of the load and over a period of time, the share of the load taken by customer increases and the share of the consultant's load reduces. A typical project will look like this.

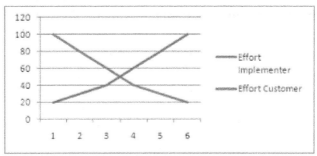

Normal ERP Implementations

In this case the load of the project shifts from the implementer to the customer somewhere in the middle of the Project. Usually this happens after CRP 2 Demo and before the CRP 3 demo. From the breakeven point onwards, the customer take the responsibility for the delivery of correct data, correcting the implementers process understanding and helping the implementation consultant. After the breakeven point, the implementation teams effort will gradually reduce as shown in the above figure or in some projects will remain at higher level for some time, while the implementation consultant is hand holding the customer user.

However, there can be two major deviations to the above chart. In the first case, the breakeven point is reached much earlier in the cycle. This is very good for the project since, customer is taking the project load very early in the implementation cycle. Such projects invariably are highly successful with delivery of very high quality and the end result is a very satisfied customer. The chart relating to a successful project is shown below.

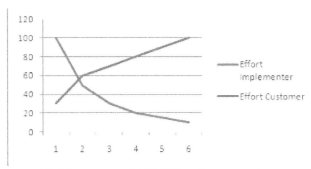

Highly successful ERP implementations

In the above chart, the load of implementation has shifted to the customer in the month 2 itself.

What are the factors which enable to transfer the load to the customer very early in the project?

First one is the knowledge of the consultant. Any ERP implementation is only as good as the weakest consultant in the team. To successfully implement ERP, it is very important to choose the best consultants. They may be expensive, but the expense is worth the benefit that you will get from a timely and successful implementation. The consultant is very knowledgeable about the customer's business, understands customer's pains and also provides multiple options for any of the issues that the customer may be facing. The customer user on the other hand is characterized by high level of intelligence and willingness to take responsibility and load in the project.

And finally, the anatomy of a failed implementation. This is characterized by very delayed breakeven point. Normally, in such type of projects, the implementation consultants will be spending time by themselves, with hardly any interaction with the customer. The testing in such projects is characterized by creation of a lot of 'TESTCUST', 'TESTITEMS' etc, with the consultant hardly understanding the business of the customer. Normally, the implementation consultant will not be aware of the customer's business and will be a novice / amateur in the use of the application. The chart below shows the life-cycle of such a project.

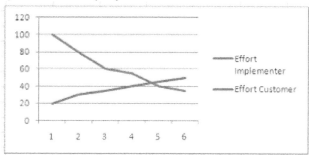

Failed ERP Implementations

You can be sure that in such projects we will have finally a very disgruntled and unhappy customer.

That is it !! My views on how to implement a successful project. Hopefully you would have learned something from my experience. Pl. note that above reflect my views and is not based on any scientific concepts of Project Management.

Requirement gathering: The pain in a consultant's life

"How do you prepare tea?"
"Well, we boil some water, put some sugar, add some milk, add some tea, put this powder and boil it all till it becomes tea".
"What is that powder?"
"We don't know."
"Then why are you adding it?"
"Because our mom used to add it?"
"Why did your mom add it?"
"We don't know."
In the world of requirement gathering, this is a scene one comes up so often. Here is an example.
"How do you create a purchase order?"
"Well first we note down the details of the requirement, take a printout, get it approved and then enter the PO in the legacy system",
"Why do you get the PO approved and then enter in the system?"
"I think it is because....... well I don't know, I have always done it this way"
Or another,
"What are you expecting from the system?"
"We have many warehouses in the city. We need warehouse wise trial balance"
"Why do you need warehouse wise trial balance? do you track assets at each warehouse"

"No, but we are currently doing it this way and we want the system to provide that"

Requirement gathering can be one of the most frustrating part of an ERP Consultant's life. Especially if you are sitting with users who 'add the powder while making tea' without knowing why she is doing that way. They follow a process because they have been doing it that way since they started working. Can the system meet their requirements?

Unfortunately many consultants also end up providing whatever the user asks for without probing further without knowing the real reason for these requirements. Many a times it is due to the lack of business knowledge on the part of the consultants. Most of the ERP functional consultants join the IT industry immediately after graduation without having a feel of how the business functions. Through practice they become very comfortable with the application and end up providing whatever the client asks for in a bid to please the customer. For instance, in the 'Trial Balance for warehouse' scenario mentioned above, one of the consultants came out with the idea of creating each warehouse as a 'company' segment value in Oracle. On deeper probing it was found that what the user wanted was 'warehouse wise profitability' which he had confused with 'trial balance'

He was making tea without knowing why he was adding the 'special powder'

PS: On deeper probing it was found that their mom used to add the special powder because they were living in a cold weather and the special powder had a way of invigorating the body.

Analytical V/s Transactional Information in an ERP Implementation

Based on the type of decisions they help to make, information can be divided into two types. One, **analytical information** and two, **transactional information**. Analytical information is a derived information. This information is derived (summarized, detailed, complemented) from the information that you enter in the transaction system. Analytical information help the organization to analyse the data. This is used mostly by managers and senior management in making managerial and strategic decisions. For example, a trend of purchase price of a raw material is an example of analytical information. Normally you do not take a business decision (like increasing the selling price) based on a single jump in the procurement price. Analytical information might ultimately end up generating a transaction decision (organization deciding to increase the selling price) but the main purpose of the analytical information is to help the organization analyse the transactional data.

Transactional information on the other hand is an information which help to take a decision in the current transaction. This is mostly used for making decisions at the operator level. For example, checking of quality samples is a transaction information. Based on an output of quality testing, the organization may decide to discard a production run altogether. The decisions based on transaction information is short term and immediate and alter the flow of the transaction. In jewellery industry for example, any change in the procurement price is reflected in a change in selling price. In this example, the procurement price of gold is a transactional information.

The above is depicted in the diagram below.

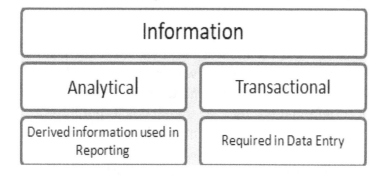

The above differentiation has implications in ERP solution design. First of all, a consultant should know if a particular requirement relate to data input or analysis. This decision is easy in case of some information and for others will need judgement from the consultant. If it is related to data input, it is probably a transactional information and the system should be configured to capture the information. Take the requirement for 'Product Segment wise profitability' for example. This requirement implies that the information on product segment should be captured in all the sales and material transactions and the same should flow to GL. This is an example of transactional information. System should be designed to capture this information in all the relevant transactions. Since analytical information is used to for analysis and reporting, it need not impact the transactional flow and hence need not be configured in the system. For example, if fluctuation in Procurement price is an analytical information, every single fluctuation need not be captured in the item cost. You can design a report that will provide the analytical data that you want from the above information.

Unfortunately this does not happen in real life implementations. A consultant who creates a GL flex field to capture the customer master is converting an analytical information into a transactional purpose. Another example could be that of a consultant increasing the number of balancing segment because client wanted 'Product (or State) wise trial balance'. Or that of a consultant designing an elaborate procedure to provide accurate 'average' price based on every little fluctuation in Procurement price.

Transaction information, as mentioned above, impacts decisions relating to the flow of transactions. Normally, the system should be designed to capture this type of information. Remember that the transaction information will most likely be used for analytical purposes, but the chance of analytical information being used for transaction purposes is very rare.

Let me illustrate this difference with another example typical in a manufacturing industry. Let us say that the customer has two production lines (Line 1 and Line 2) to produce the same product. Both lines are identical in nature. The requirement is to capture Line wise efficiency. How do you do it?

The transactional approach is to create two separate routings for the same product. When you create a production order, select the correct routing and proceed. This is a simple solution, configured by most consultants.

There are problems with this approach. Some products allow only one 'Active' routing. If this is the case, then you will have to complicate the above solution by adding a customization to 'activate' the selected line and 'deactivate' the other.

See how the solution is becoming more and more complex?

The analytical (and leaner) approach will be to create a single routing, and enter line number as an additional information while creating a new production order. This enables you to get the required information, 'Line wise efficiency', while keeping the solution leaner and efficient.

(This is an example from one of the projects that I had worked on)

As a consultant, it is very important for you to differentiate the information requirement into the transactional and analytical categories. This will help you in creating an optimum, leaner and efficient solution.

INDIA
LOCALIZATION

TDS Flow in Accounts Payable - Oracle Apps India Localization

Introduction

Organizations are expected to withhold a percentage of the payments that they make to their suppliers and remit the amount thus collected with the tax authorities at the end of every specified period. This process is known as Withholding Tax or Tax Deducted at source.

The suppliers in turn receive a certificate to the extent of the amounts thus remitted and they will file the same with the Tax Authorities as a part of their Income tax declaration.
While withholding tax calculation in majority of countries is effective at the time of making payments to the suppliers, in India the Tax Deducted at Source (TDS) is effective at the time of accepting the supplier invoice itself. This makes the tax calculation, management and tracking of TDS much more complicated.

This document discusses an end-to-end scenario, where the TDS is calculated at the time of entering a supplier advance (Prepayment) and netting off the same against the invoices entered in the Oracle Applications Accounts Payable module.

1. When prepayment invoice is generated in AP.

In Oracle Apps, you enter a Supplier Prepayment as a Supplier Invoice of type 'Prepayment'. In this example, we are entering a prepayment of Rs.55000. Accounting entry generated is as follows.

| Prepaid Expenses A/c | Debit | 55000 |
| Liability | Credit | 55000 |

2. System Creates TDS Credit Memo on supplier (Assuming 10% is the rate)

At the time of validating the above invoice, the system creates two additional documents. One, it creates a credit memo on the supplier (discussed in this step) and two, it creates a TDS invoice on the Tax Authority, thus moving the Tax from the supplier to the Tax Authority (discussed in step 3 below). For this purpose, Tax Authority has to be created as a Supplier in the ERP system

In this example, TDS rate of 10% is assumed.

| Liability | Debit | 5000 |
| TDS Control A/c | Credit | 5000 |

The rate gets picked up from the tax master where we have defined the tax as type 'Tax Deducted at Source'.

3. System Creates TDS Invoice on IT Authority (TDS Supplier)

This is already discussed above.

TDS Control A/c	Debit	5000
Liability	Credit	5000

4. Making the payment to the supplier on the prepayment invoice created above.

You will net off both the prepayment invoice (step 1) and the credit memo (step 2) when making the payment to the supplier.

Liability	Debit	49500
Cash A/c	Credit	49500

5. Making the payment to the tax authority on the TDS Invoice

Liability	Debit	5500
Cash A/c	Credit	5500

6. Enter Standard Invoice on Supplier (Raising invoice of 40000)

Here we are entering a standard invoice on the supplier and netting it off with the prepayment created above. The invoice amount is Rs. 40000. At the time of validating this invoice, the system will create TDS Credit Memo and TDS Invoice as discussed previously (Steps 2 and 3).

Accounting entry for the invoice.

Expense A/c	Debit	40000
Liability	Credit	40000

7. TDS Credit Memo on the above invoice

Liability	Debit	4000
TDS Control A/c	Credit	4000

8. TDS invoice on IT Authority

TDS Control A/c	Debit	4000
Liability	Credit	4000

9. Attaching Prepayment created above to the current invoice.

Liability	Debit	40000
Prepaid Expenses A/c	Credit	40000

10. TDS Return Invoice on supplier to reverse the original TDS Credit memo on the Prepayment.

This is a bit complicated to explain. If you make payment to the tax authority on this TDS invoice (created in Step 8), you would have made a total payment of 5500+4000 to the tax authority. This is wrong. Actually you don't have to pay anything on this invoice since you have already paid the TDS on the prepayment. To reverse the TDS Credit memo and the TDS Invoice created above (in step 7 and 8), the system creates a Reversal Invoice on the supplier and a Credit memo on the tax authority to the extent of Rs.4000

| TDS Control A/c | Debit | 4000 |
| Liability | Credit | 4000 |

11. TDS Return Credit Memo on IT Authority to reverse the Original TDS Invoice on the Prepayment

| Liability | Debit | 4000 |
| TDS Control A/c | Credit | 4000 |

Note that TDS Control A/c is an intermediate account which gets netted off at the end of a TDS Credit Memo and a TDS Invoice. This account is set up when you set up the tax master.

This is diagrammatically explained in the table below.

Step	Description	Debit / Credit	Prepaid Expenses	Liability	TDS Control	Expenses	Cash
1	Enter prepayment	Debit	55000				
		Credit		-55000			
2	TDS Credit Memo on Vendor	Debit		5500			
		Credit			-5500		
3	TDS Invoice on Tax Authority	Debit			5500		
		Credit		-5500			
4	Vendor Payment	Debit		49500			
		Credit					-49500
5	Payment to Tax Authority	Debit		5500			
		Credit					-5500
6	Supplier Invoice	Debit				40000	
		Credit		-40000			
7	TDS Credit Memo on Vendor	Debit		4000			
		Credit			-4000		
8	TDS Invoice on Tax Authority	Debit			4000		
		Credit		-4000			
9	Prepayment Setoff with	Debit		40000			
		Credit	-40000				

GENERAL

Key skills of a good ERP consultant

In my opinion, an ERP Consultant should have the following personality traits.

1. Listening Skills: The key trait that separates a good consultant from an average consultant is his / her listening skills. A good listener will be able to pinpoint the issues being raised by the customer and thereby provide the solution to the real problems of the customer. A good listener will most often use the 'Why' word a lot. A consultant who is not a good listener will most often end up in providing generic solution rather than providing specific solution to the issues faced by the customer. An average consultant can be heard using the phrase 'This is how the product works, you have to change the process'.

2. Closure skills: Most of the average consultants will provide almost complete solution, but fail to close the issue. This will lead to festering issues which will come to haunt you in the most critical times. Most of the time the closure can be achieved with a simple three line minutes of the meeting. However, I am surprised at the number of consultants who lack closure skills. Lack of closure skills is related to the third aspect of a good consultant, which is communication skills.

3. Communication Skills: While listening skills play a very important part in the initial stages of the project, this is only a part of the overall communications skills. There are three aspects to the communication skills. They are Listening Skills, Presentation Skills and Idea Selling skills. Presentation skills can be oral and written presentation. The communication skills should not be confused with ability to talk confidently. Communication skills relate to the ability to separate data from information, coming to very common sense root causes, and finding innovative solutions and finally convincing the customer about the strength of your solution. I have seen many very good consultants fail in this aspect.

4. Documentation Skills: A good consultant documents everything. Minutes of the meeting, summary of discussions, strategies, plans, designs, user guides... every thing is documented. Not only they document everything, they also get closure by getting their documents formally accepted by the customer.

5. People Skills: ERP implementation is nothing but a people management process. In the beginning of the project you have a skeptical and probably scared user from the customer side. It is the consultant's duty to make the user confident in the product and the solutioning so that at the end of the day she can add value to the implementation. Many a consultant fail in this aspect since they do not put the necessary time and effort to understand the customer user.

6. Business Knowledge: It is a no brainer that the

implementation consultant should have the knowledge of business. What does this imply? It implies two aspects. One, knowledge of business, industry, statutory regulations etc and two, the detailed knowledge of the customer's business. Many a times the consultant goes thru a 10 months of implementation without having a clue on the customer's business or products. And that will lead to a bad implementation. I normally ask the following questions to understand the customers business. How many plants do you have, Which plant produces the most? What is the spread of production load between the plants? What product groups do you have? What is the most profitable product? Who is the most profitable customer? Who is the customer with most revenue for you? What are the raw materials? How do you do production planning? How do you manage inventory?. The idea is to understand the key pain areas of a business and try to address those pains in your implementation.

Every job has to be done twice.....

As per the book '7 Habits of highly effective people', you have to do every task twice.

Either you plan the task thoroughly, thereby first 'doing' the task in your mind, and go and act your plan, or go without planning, do the task, commit errors and redo the same.

This means,

Either you do once in your mind and once actually, or

Either do once actually, commit errors, and do the same task again correcting the errors.

Either way, you do it twice.

But the second approach has its pitfalls.

One, you might permanently damage the thing that you are working on. For example, if you are filling a light bulb and it falls down and breaks, then you cannot do that task again. Only option is to spend dark night.

Two, You might temporarily damage it to the extent that it has become useless.

Three, You might face unanticipated pitfalls.

Somehow, going to do a task without proper planning is a norm rather than exception in ERP implementation scenario.

Consider my friend X going to collect requirements. He goes in without a plan. He has not prepared on the customer's business. He does not know the key revenue and cost drivers of the business. He does not know who are the members of the team that is going to attend the session from the customer side and he does not have any idea of the roles played by the people who have come to give him the requirements. He is not aware if the people that are giving the requirements are the same people who are going to support in his implementation.

Totally unplanned.....

So what happened in the meeting?

The key information was not received, and this gap was identified only when the team was configuring the solution. By that time the key resource who was to have given this information had moved to a new division and it took about two weeks, a lot of conflicts between the customer and the team and a loss of momentum in the project before the complete requirements were received.

This means.....

Mr.X went to collect requirements without a plan and had to do the same process again at a loss of money, time and motivation.

On the other hand, every time Mr.Y goes to collect the requirements he plans it perfectly. First of all he plans the physical infrastructure very carefully. He will know where the meeting will be held and he would ensure that all the basic requirements including projector and whiteboard, markers, duster all are ensured for the meeting. He will have a clear prior information on the participants in the meeting, and what are their roles and contributions in the meeting as well as in the ongoing project. He will know the internal power structure of the customer team attending the meeting. He will have a clear idea of the important and mandatory information that he will require to collect. If possible, he will prepare a questionnaire to collect all the mandatory information.

And he will communicate.....

He will constantly interact with his customer contact as to what are the important information that the customer thinks is important. He will ask key questions like What are the key concerns of the customer? What is the overall objective of the customer from this meeting? What are the individual objectives of each of the participants from the meeting?

Even before he speaks the first word in the formal session, he has already ran thru the sessions in his mind and he is ready with all the important questions and clarifications that make the requirement gathering session so successful. Every stakeholder including the customer, the customer Project Manager and his own team are all satisfied with the outcome of the meeting.

As you can see, both Mr.X and Mr.Y had to do the requirement gathering process twice. Only difference is that at the end of the session Mr.X had a frustrated stakeholder team while Mr. Y had an extremely satisfied stakeholder team.

Any guesses as to whose project will end up successfully?

Document Change History

No	Date	Name	From Edition	To Edition	Change Details
1	08-May-19	V K Ramaswamy	None	1.0	
2	13-May-19	V K Ramaswamy	1.0	2.0	Spelling errors addressed. Formatting done